Intersection and Beyond, Volume II

Intersection and Beyond

Volume II

by

Elizabeth Boyden Howes

Guild for Psychological Studies
Publishing House
San Francisco

Published in the United States of America by
The Guild for Psychological Studies Publishing House
2230 Divisadero Street
San Francisco, California 94115

Cover Art: Susan Renfrew
Cover Design: Dorothy Nissen
Typesetting and Layout: PAN Typesetters, Eugene, Oregon

Library of Congress Cataloging in Publication Data

Howes, Elizabeth Boyden, 1907
  Intersection and Beyond.

  Includes indexes.
  1. Psychology and religion — Addresses, essays, lectures. 2. Psycho-
analysis and religion — Addresses, essays, lectures. I. Title.
BF51.H64   1986   201'.9   86-3067
ISBN 0-917479-04-1   (pbk. : v.1)
ISBN 0-917479-07-6   (pbk. : v.2)

Dedication

To the many persons in seminars and analysands — persons from the Judaic tradition and the Christian tradition (Catholic, Anglican, and Protestant)—who in dialogue have helped to clarify the conceptual development in this book.

Contents

Introduction

This second volume of *Intersection and Beyond*, which continues the format of the first volume, consists of ten lectures given by me over the last ten years. These lectures represent a conceptual and experiential development of the basic ideas set forth in the first volume, yet it is complete in itself. They represent the core of the work of the seminars held under the auspices of the Guild for Psychological Studies. These seminars work with the life and teachings of Jesus in the synoptic Gospels, and their mythic and depth psychological content. The text used is *Records of the Life of Jesus* by Henry B. Sharman.

Because they were originally lectures, and not papers written specifically for publication, they have a somewhat informal style. Also, because these lectures were given at different times and at different places, there is inevitably repetition of thought and quotations.

The panel discussion on "Darkness and Gods," Chapter 9, was presented by Luella Sibbald, Sheila Moon, and myself, the three founding leaders of the Guild for Psychological Studies.

The two lectures on the "Kingdom of God and the Self," Chapter 2, were presented by myself and Jeanne Hendrickse, Ph.D. Jeanne Hendrickse is originally from South Africa, and came to the United States by way of the World Council of Churches. She is now an active member of the Guild leadership group and is engrossed with social and religious problems.

The first lecture was dedicated to Dorothy Phillips, because of her specific contribution to the activities in Claremont. Due to illness she could not be present.

I have felt encouraged to publish this second volume because of the response to the first volume and the response at the moment to each of these lectures.

God, Self, Ego, and Choice

"Man was created for the sake of choice" is a statement from the Jewish mystical tradition. We were created for the sake of choice. The same tradition also states that everything is already determined by God at birth, except whether a person will be righteous or not. We might say that everything is decided except whether that person will or will not *choose* to become conscious. Aldous Huxley puts this point succinctly, "The Choice Is Always Ours."

What do these statements say? On the one hand, the purpose of creation, of the Creator, or of the evolutionary pattern making for meaning is clear. Choice is wanted, but not guaranteed. There is a *margin of freedom* from the beginning that allows for, even demands, creative decision from each of us. The central core—choice—lies within the human sphere.

But a choice of what? A choice for what? Out of what does it come? Why do we refuse basic choice? Why do we accept it? Where is the makeweight? No one has stated this more clearly than Jesus of Nazareth. He said there are two ways for us to follow: There is the narrow gate and the strait way which leads to life, and there is the wide gate and the broad way which leads to destruction; and few be they that find the way to life.

These are the matters in my heart and mind that I hope we may ponder together. These concerns have always been central to me; but I speak today with a tremendous sense of urgency. None of us can afford to be casual, nonchalant, or indifferent about the ecological threat to our planet or the threat of nuclear destruction.

* Presented at the Claremont Jung Club, Claremont, California, November 7, 1982.

Something has gone terribly wrong. After millions of years of development, both of earth and of the human psyche, we face the possibility—through choice or nonchoice—of total extinction.

As Jonathan Schell has said in his excellent book, *The Fate of the Earth*:

> At present most of us do nothing. We are silent. We remain calm. We take refuge in the hope that the holocaust won't happen. We deny the truth around us. We drowse our way to the end of the world. But if we could once shake off our lethargy and fatigue and begin to act, the climate would begin to change.

In the Hopi creation myth one of the main deities, Spider Grandmother, says, "Only those who forget *why* they came into the world will lose their way." We have lost our way to a frightening degree. We may not be able to save the planet, but we can choose whether or not to try.

Over many years I have become increasingly convinced that the basic mythic inward truths that dominated the life of Jesus have a value greater than and distinct from the developed Christian myth, and that these truths have been greatly illumined by insights of the analytical psychology of C. G. Jung. The title of this talk, "God, Self, Ego, and Choice," supersedes the original title, which was "Ego, Self, God, and Choice." I came to the conviction that the ego, in its full religious meaning as a latecomer on the evolutionary scene, can only be grasped if we have the background of Self and God. I chose to make this clear in my title.

I will speak first of God. What can we—what dare we—say about the reality behind that word? The creator God is the He/She, the God/Goddess, who is the center of all religious myth and religious teaching. There is a universal reality, a process, a "cry" (in the words of Kazantzakis), something in the universe that makes for meaning, integration, and pattern. This patterning is found in the smallest atoms and the largest galaxies. And there is also something in the universe that makes for destruction and disintegration.

This will to meaning, this "desire," in the words of Jacob Boehme, is defined as the nothing desiring to become Something (the fire and the longing), and is the *a priori* existent reality in the universe. It is the Eternal that wants to come into time, into manifestation. In the words of Martin Buber, the "Thou" expresses Itself in all situations if there is an I to confront it.

The seed that falls onto the ground has no choice but to become what is meant to grow out of that kind of seed. But we are the one seed in God's ground that does have a choice, and that is a serious matter. In the Hebrew Scriptures we see the God that wants covenant with people, and this God includes all possible opposites: Him/Her, love/wrath, life/destruction, wounding/healing. In Lamentations, we find, "From the mouth of the Most High come good and evil"; and from Isaiah, "I form the light and create darkness," and "I wound and I heal." The Judaic-Christian myth of the Garden of Eden includes the Tree of the Knowledge of Good and Evil as well as the Tree of Life. All these opposites within the process of God do not come to a point of integration unless a human being helps that integration, the birth of focused consciousness that grows from the potential consciousness in the God process. This God with a will for the third point of consciousness marches through history, collective and personal, constantly presenting us with alternatives to which we respond. In this sense, it is a situational God.

The Will of God becomes the deepest, richest, best value that can be discovered at all moments, out of all possible alternatives, by a human committed to choice. When that value is not actualized it is lost. The Now becomes everything.

This God is described through the Midrash prayer where God prays to Himself, "May it be my will that my love overcome my wrath." The prayer does not say, "May my love overcome my wrath"; it says, "May it be my *will* that my love overcome my wrath." The ambivalence is there at the center of the matter, but the longing is there for a new emergence out of the opposites. This does not do away with the opposites, but fulfills the longing of the opposites to be healed. As we shall see, this potential for healing comes out of the world lying within the Self.

In addition to this God moving in history, this God is also forming my destiny by being at work within my psyche and in the psyches of all of us. This is the Kingdom of God within, which Jung helps us to rediscover. This center, this Self within, has been given many names throughout history by the great mystics, the great artists, and the great religious figures. This Self is the central archetype of meaning and purposive principle within us. It is the locus *within* the psyche immanently, of the operation of the God process of opposites with the thrust towards consciousness. Therefore it partakes of the freedom of God. We may be speaking here of the function of the Holy Spirit as a connective link between the divine and the human which, in his Baptism experience, was the enlivening of the Self in Jesus and therefore in others. Because the Self reflects God, it must have everything of the opposites—light/dark, good/evil, masculine/feminine—within it. We speak of the Self as the image of God, or being made in the image of God; but what God? *How inclusive?* In our Christian tradition the Self archetype has been projected and identified with the figure of the Christ.

This Self, the image of God within, is never to be confused with God. It is God's abode inwardly, but is not the same as God. It is my impression, formed in several talks with Jung, that he never made that confusion, but some of his followers come very close. What is in the Self is very precious, and it is of great value as a reflection in the psyche and in the substance of the spirit beyond it. It is the possibility of the God of whom we have been speaking becoming incarnate in the psyche. Because of the identification of the Self with the Christ, Jung raises the question of whether the Christ image is big enough for the Self—whether, indeed, a radical change is needed for the Christ image to be all inclusive. For Jesus to do and live what he did, his inner Source as the Self or Christ-consciousness must have been larger.

There is also in the unconscious a large reservoir of hidden dynamic realities, the archetypes, which express themselves in images and symbols—the father and mother archetype, the child, the shadow, the idea of the journey, death/rebirth, the monster and the savior, the redeemer, and so on. But at the center of them all is this *holy thing* that we call the Self, the divine, which wants to come into manifestation in each individual.

The great mystic Angelus Silesius says, "Unmanifested God comes into time to be that which he never was through all eternity." The paradox is that this Self is there from birth *in potentia*. It is a given, but we realize its full meaning only when the ego is there. Throughout our lifetime this Self may be expressed in vital religious experiences, in experiences of nature, and in love; but for it to become the source of meaningful existence requires work. This is the opus, the work, whereby the fullness of the Godhead sacrifices itself through a limitation to come into the human. The potential consciousness within that process comes into an interior dwelling place where the potential may be actualized.

What have I been saying up to now? That there is a purposive, transcendent reality, consisting of light and dark and all opposites, that moves in history and gives us alternatives, choices of freedom. This reality is immanently present in the psyche, with the Self as its dwelling place, where the tension of the opposites, outside and inside, is the balanced and centered longing for integration. *To fulfill this longing, the human is created for choice.*

We come, then, to the ego—indispensable for this integration—and the challenge of its religious function. If the Self is understood as the center of the total personality, conscious and unconscious, the ego is the center of the conscious personality, differentiated from the unconscious but not split off from it, and also separate from the outer world but related to it. The creative I is concerned with value choices in the complexity of possibilities. It therefore has a moral quality, and, paradoxically, it must be spontaneous and deliberate. It is the thrust of the Self, the arm of the Self, that can choose; it is the choicemaker on which everything depends. We can misuse it destructively, or we can create a beautiful world for ourselves, our community, and perhaps even for God. The Self is there at birth, as has been said, but the ego develops within the specific history of each person. One can choose the value of self-discovery for creation and integration, outer and inner, or one can choose for negativity and destruction in very subtle ways. This is the freedom of the ego, its ambivalence, its anguish, and its blessing.

Why one person responds with fullness to real choice by the ego and another does not remains a mystery. There are a few beautiful lines of poetry from the Christmas oratorio by W. H. Auden, "For the Time Being":

Today the unknown seeks the known
What I am willed to ask
Your own will has to answer
Child, it lies within your power of choosing
To conceive the child who chooses you.

What is this saying? If we are once touched by something, if the hand has been on our shoulder, if the stars have crossed the horizon in a certain pattern, if we have been chosen by destiny, then the birth is up to us. Each individual carries the potential of being awakened. The time between conception and birth is long and arduous, but eminently worthwhile. And the fruits of both the big and little steps of transformation are constantly there, bestowing courage, perseverance, joy, and meaningful suffering. Recently, while gathering small melons and gold and yellow pumpkins from our garden, it came to me that this was like an ingathering of a harvest of authentic living. There is a harvest of different colors all along the way.

Once, in a personal conversation with Dr. Jung, he spoke of the need of the ego for willpower to turn to the task of transformation. I was interested in Jung's use of that term, which we do not use much today—willpower. At one place in his writings Jung speaks of will as "energy freely disposable to the psyche as opposed to being chained to instinct and complex." Thus the choice is there for our overarching decision and for the work of transformation, not once but throughout our lifetime. This will determine whether we remain static, bound in unwholesome patterns, or become free, flexible, and responsive.

Most of us are comparatively good people. We aren't out committing murder. But it is overwhelmingly clear that our negativity and darkness, our shadow, controls in subtle ways, and becomes apparent in the problem of hostility, violence, and pettiness between groups and between individuals.

Yes, the evil in the world today is clear. What is *not* clear—and needs to be—is that the responsibility lies with each one of us to recognize how we contribute to this infectiousness from our unsolved, dark side of life. Animals, trees, weather—such things naturally cannot choose, except in a most rudimentary form. But the human ego can choose; it can choose to sow seed for growth, or it can choose to poison its own ground. The ego facing options is most demanding, because we would like to say everything is determined. But there is this margin of freedom, even in regard to attitudes in exacting and imprisonment situations. This was made clear, for example, in the writings of Victor Frankel, in his description of the difference in the attitudes of the various concentration camp inmates and their approach to that which they were encountering.

Out of the myriad of possibilities that outer situations and the inner unconscious offer, and out of the work of detaching the ego from identification with situations while remaining related to them, the individual develops his or her own personality. What we speak of today as the ego-Self axis refers to the "I" that is connected to its deep source and then is able to respond to the "Thou" manifest in outer situations. Here the real "I" serves the greater "Thou," outward and inward. The work of how this "I" developed is beyond what can be dealt with here.

Perhaps this additional contribution of Jung's will help us. He has written, "Only the person who has renounced his/her ego-bound intention for a supra-personal value can be said to be serving a king." Whereas egocentricity refers to the process where the ego has become the center; ego-bound intentions refer to the situation where the ego is still attached to good intentions, to goals, to causes or ideas, or to people who once were good to serve. It can become an attachment that needs to be changed into a creative detachment.

Perhaps it is the function of prayer and meditation, as distinct from analysis, to reaffirm the ego's direction and function and choice at its very core, because it is easy for

the ego to become inflated by contamination of unconscious powers or to lose the sense of choice by becoming rigidly determined and one-sidedly ethical, or to grow
lazy and lethargic. The new ethic required must be much
more inclusive than our old set of rigid rules of behavior.
And this requires us to be very awake.

Now why is this choice so difficult? And what role has
the Church or Christianity played in making it so difficult?
This in no way belittles the Church, which continues to be
a container for the journey for millions of people. However,
for many, the search for religious living and the
God/human dialogue is no longer contained in churches,
thus creating demands for new forms. True religious and
deeply held cherished beliefs prevent us, I believe, from
taking real responsibility for our lives; and they also tend
to keep us from taking the inner world seriously, and limit
our perception of the actualities of the outer world. First,
we have let Jesus, as Jesus Christ, carry our journey, and
we worship him.

The negative side is that although dogma has its value,
it tends to keep us from our own individual direct religious
experiences of creative depths. Then belief takes the place
of our own creativity. By putting the authority that Jesus
was talking about outside us, we have deprived ourselves
of the indwelling authority that we so desperately need. We
have failed to accomplish our own journey of working on
our own defensiveness, egocentricity, transformation of
our shadow side, and taking our wounds seriously enough
to help the creative healing process.

In the great Navajo myth "Where the Two Came to
Their Father," the twin heros are constantly being helped
in all their meetings with the monsters to make right
choices. They are helped in dealing with the monsters by
such creatures as Little Wind, Inch Worm, and Spider
Woman—all very small creatures, unobtrusive but wise,
and on the side of healing and wholeness. We haven't
found these healing forces enough inside ourselves. They
are there, certainly, as part of our God process.

Jung writes in *The Secret of the Golden Flower*, "The
imitation of Christ has forever this disadvantage. We worship a divine model and fail to make real this meaning in

our own lives. If Jesus had done this he would have re-
mained a respectable carpenter.''

We have made Jesus the chooser, and he has become
the object of belief; thus we do not participate in our own
journey. In this sense Jesus has carried the ego/Self archetype by the projection of him into the Christ, and has not
been taken enough into ourselves. I might add here that I
find many people today, deep in the Jungian tradition,
who will say they are not following Jesus as any divine
model, but feel they are rejecting it in favor of some
Eastern approach, or at least by leaving the Church. Very
often, however, analysis reveals the depth to which the
archetypes behind Christian beliefs and dogmas are helpful if people are fully conscious of the inner symbols. It is
when we remain unconscious of their meanings that stag-
nation occurs. One wonders whether this is part of what
happened to the Christian myth. Jung has said, "Christianity slumbers and has neglected to develop its myth further in the course of centuries . . . the myth has become
mute and gives no answers.''

What values might we find in the Gospels if we do not
stop with Jesus and his value, but rather continue to
understand his awareness of his mythical sources, and
open ourselves to the sources within each of us? The
universality of the basic mythic motifs of death/rebirth,
virginal birth, the wounded healer, and the savior/
redeemer archetype are all clearly lived and stated by
Jesus as archetypes to which he related inwardly, but
which he did not identify with. If we do not move through
Jesus and his life to what was behind him, we leave something untouched. The term "moving through" may not be
the best phrase, but it is the only one I can use to describe
what I mean by moving through to the Source behind.

The English author John Middleton Murray once
wrote, "Jesus is in our bones. We must get him out of our
bones and accept him or reject him consciously." Many
theologians and many Jungians stop short of this. They
stay within the incompleteness of the Christian faith and
do not explore the depth of the wisdom *behind* Jesus'
teachings. We need to remember that Jesus did not say to
follow him, but to follow God. Jung has said, "Christianity

is a great moral achievement but individuation is greater. Individuation is to discover, live out of the deepest potential Self within us." The synoptic Gospels are full of this message of Jesus' teaching of the way to life, and his own struggle with archetypal powers and not with the later Christian myth of Jesus as Savior.

Moreover, another concept that has made creative choice so difficult, besides the projection onto Jesus, is the separation that is generally held in Christianity between light and dark. This has confined the concept of God and the Christ or Redeemer to the light and masculine side. We have forgotten the truth of Psalm 139, "If I make my bed in heaven, Thou art there and if I make my bed in hell, Thou art there." Jesus served this God of opposites, especially the inclusion of good and evil. But in Christianity in general, and for the Christ image expressing the Self, the emphasis has been on the light and perfect side. There are, of course, great exceptions to this. Perfection excludes imperfection, and wholeness includes both. Few problems are more prominent today for analysts than the struggle of people to be perfect, or the struggle to avoid guilt because they are not perfect. In another translation, the word for perfect is "you shall be all-inclusive" (Matt 5:48). This means total inclusion of all of our parts. What Jesus did in the inclusion of evil is a very different picture of what his God-source and his messianic image within contained, out of which his word and his living came. Paraphasing Matt. 7:35, he said, "Don't put the beam in the other fellow's eye and think that you have only a mote in your own. But look at the beam or the log in your own, work at it, and then you will be able to see to take the speck out of the other's eye." We project all we don't like and certainly all we don't know onto other people, groups, and nations. The intensity of these individual projections then become world problems. Very few people have made a stronger or a clearer statement on projection than Jesus.

Jesus also said "Resist not evil" (Matt. 5:39). Not to turn away from, not to be defensive about, not to identify with; but rather, not to resist. To be able to take evil into our own hands and to work with this transformation. We

are reminded again of Jung's statement, "We lack imagination in evil." And that is one of our great problems today: We lack imagination in evil, both individually and
socially. We may lack it because we have never really
taken it into our arms for transformation.

In another situation, Jesus speaks of how defilement
comes from within us, not from outside. It comes from the
heart in the form of evil thoughts, pride, adultery, fornica-
tion, murder, and theft. These come from the heart. And
the first commandment, "Thou shalt love the Lord thy
God with all thy heart, soul, strength, and mind," must
mean to include loving God with our evil also. Erich
Neumann points out in *Depth Psychology and the New
Ethic* that the translation of the first commandment in the
Hasidic tradition is, "Thou shalt love God with the whole
heart," meaning "thou shalt love God with both thy good
and evil inclinations." Jesus was a realist. He knew the
way of darkness because he knew the nature of God and of
humans. Jesus says, "Be not therefore anxious for the
morrow: . . . Sufficient unto the day is the evil thereof"
(Matt. 6:34). There is enough potential evil each day within
and outside to take care of. We might also add, sufficient
unto the day is the good thereof—"the surprises of grace,"
as Meister Eckhart called them. The evil may attack us
from the inside, from our own deepest, negative side, if we
are not cognizant of its dynamic. It may attack and affect
us in other social forms of violence, hostility, and racial
tension. The whole ecological crisis caused by the rape of
our earth will affect us; and poverty, injustice, and inequality will come upon us in unbidden ways.

The exclusion of the feminine in our religious culture is
becoming increasingly clear, and so are the symptoms
manifested from this omission. Much thought is being
given to language change, and change in church forms into
feminine emphases and concerns. But we need also to go
deeper into the feminine meanings, attitudes, and qualities
in the Godhead, in our own cultures, and in ourselves. The
goddess needs to be redeemed from exile, because we do
find Her in our Greek, Judaic, and pagan roots. She needs
to be honored as part of the totality, because She brings a

rootedness, Love, and all-inclusiveness. This is not easy for us to do, whether we are men or women, but it is absolutely imperative.

A quote from one of Jung's letters speaks to both of these points—of how we let Jesus carry our journey, and of our refusal to look at darkness. I think it is clear that darkness is not to be equated with evil, but also represents the unknown and not yet seen. This is to me one of Jung's most biting and wonderful letters, and I would like to paraphrase some of it.

To a minister:

> We place ourselves under *his* cross, but by golly not under our own. The cross of Christ was *borne by himself* and was *his*. To put oneself under somebody else's cross, which has already been carried by him, is certainly easier than to carry your own cross amid the mockery and contempt of the world. That way you remain nicely ensconced in tradition and are praised as devout. Have your congregation understood that they must close their ears to the traditional teachings and go through the darknesses of their own souls and set aside everything in order to become that which every individual bears in himself as his individual task and that no one can take this burden from him?

This is a strong statement indeed. Because we haven't carried our journey we know that the split between light and dark still remains, and we thus have been cut off from the totality of our own inner depth and have not taken responsibility for it. Our fate from this may be nuclear disaster— seeming to me possibly to be God's darkness that we have not been aware of in our onesidedness.

This cutoffness is also shown in our lack of understanding of the meaning of symbols as the expression of totality, and in the dearth of symbols. Jung again has said, "The symbolic life is the meaningful life and the function of culture is to know the adequacy of symbols." In seminars for ministers, when they are asked what symbols move them, many or most will speak of nature symbols and symbols from other traditions. Very few speak of symbols from the Church.

We need to go down into ourselves to find the meaning of the archetypal realities that the traditional symbols represent. We also need to become aware and perceptive of what in the real outer world move us as guides to the inner processes. For example, what stories in the newspaper really grip us? We need new rituals, personally and collectively, that express the dynamic movement of the soul. We need new ways of meditation based on the structure of the Western psyche and inclusive of the various facets within. Many meditation techniques today seem to arouse the unconscious contents, but without an ego-consciousness that relates these contents to the consciousness of the person. To become a person is to work at bringing together conscious and unconscious. We are acquainted with ways of exploring the unconscious through analysis, therapy, art, nature, and dreams, but the fulfillment of the demands for total integrated living involves these other aspects. If we live on a very rational, logical, conscious level, with no relationship to what is inside, we not only deprive ourselves, but we deprive that which wants to be born inside us.

In conclusion, I would like to quote a line from the English playwright, Christopher Fry, in *Sleep of Prisoners*.

> Thank God our time is now
> when wrong comes up to face us everywhere,
> never to leave us until we take
> the longest stride of soul that Man ever took.
> Affairs are now soul-sized.
> The enterprise is exploration into God.

What kind of exploration, one asks, and what God? What's the nature of the true reality? What's the nature of a new exploration?

Jung has written, "For in the experience of the Self it is no longer the opposites of God and Man that are to be reconciled as before but rather the opposites within the God image itself." Now the God of opposites—which is the God Jesus served—of longing, of need must be found. This is nothing short of a need of a radical revision of the Christian myth. The new, honest exploration must be into the dark side of ourselves, into the difficulties that are tearing us to pieces. We need an exploration leading to self-acceptance. From the Gospel of Thomas come the words:

> If you bring forth what is within you,
> what you bring forth will save you.
> If you do not bring forth what is within you,
> What you do not bring forth will destroy you.

If we survive the nuclear threat, the new age—the Aquarian age to come—will give us a rich symbol: Each person carrying his or her own jar of water on the shoulder, with water pouring out to serve others and to help bring about genuine community between people and nations. We may contribute to a genuine peace and to the continuation of the divine experiment of the God-human dialogue. The price is very great, but the value is greater.

Perhaps my thoughts can be summarized by the dream of a person of maturity, in which the Voice said, "Stop asking who you are and start asking *whom you serve*." We are defined in our ego-Self personality by *how* we serve the Source from which we came. The choice and the struggle to bring that Source into the reality of human living is the fulfillment to the Longing that runs forever between God and human; wanting, needing a Person in which to incarnate, to enflesh the deep, divine Will.

The Kingdom of God and the Self

By Elizabeth Boyden Howes and Jeanne Hendrickse

Part I

Elizabeth Howes: In his thoughts, in his heart, in his total being, the Kingdom of God was Jesus' central vision and longing. Every word he spoke came from the Word inside, where God transcendent/manifested in history was newly born and came alive in a depth dimension. This vision, this reality, was one where people—his people and all people— would live together in a just, peaceful, flourishing society and Kingdom; one where each individual within that peace would know the experience of fulfillment and valid being. Such it was. Such he described as an invitation and a claim issuing from his people's covenant with God. Today we look at our world—not only at the most negative and awesome threat of nuclear disaster, but at a world torn by violence and hostilities, filled with injustice and inequality, poverty, and cruelty that comes from lust and the drive for power. It is a world where individual fulfillment is indeed hard to come by.

What happened to the message of Jesus? Where is it? What has Christianity done, or *not* done, with it or to it? Where is the Spirit that could reconcile and unite despite all obstacles? In these two lectures, Jeanne Hendrickse and I have chosen to examine with intense concern what Christianity has or has not done, especially in the developing nations of the Third World. In this lecture we will look

* Presented at the Guild for Psychological Studies, San Francisco, California, May 6, 1982.

at the situation, and in Lecture 2 we will search out solutions for transformation. It is a privilege for all of us to hear Jeanne, a Third World person, and one who has intensively studied the *Records of the Life of Jesus*, speak on liberation theology. Why has it arisen, and what is its meaning and challenge to us?

We feel it is no longer the time to deal with symptoms—although many courageous people are doing that—but to get at root causes. The Kingdom of God, the Reign of God, the Sovereignty of God, had for Jesus an existential quality. It is both present and, paradoxically, always coming. It is social and it is also personal. It is outer and it is inner. Its actualization did not reside in Jesus' presence. He was not the Kingdom or its fulfillment, but his teachings and their incarnation at a new level brought the possibility of its presence. At no place does Jesus refer to himself as the Center. He knew and learned a truth, but he was not that truth. If we had followed that truth and not him, we might not be at the abyss today. The Kingdom of God's fulfillment lay not only in the hands of God, but in human work and dialogic interaction with God. Jesus was concerned with many questions: When would the Kingdom come? How would it come? Who would bring it in? What would be the sign of its presence? How would it grow in individuals and in society to become a truly dynamic reality? What actually are the most significant words out of the many that he spoke from the depths of being concerning the Kingdom, and where do they come from in him? Were they from his tradition, his Jewish background, or from a newness in himself, or a combination of both?

"He that has ears to hear, let him hear . . . " (Matt. 13:9,43; Mark 4:9,23; Luke 8:8) is a refrain which we find over and over in Jesus' longest discourse on the Kingdom of God. Contrary to his people's and to John's expectation of an apocalyptic sudden appearance of the Kingdom, the parables of Jesus in this discourse emphasize a slow coming, small beginnings, and mysterious growth. The parable of the seed in the earth (Matt. 13:4-8), the parable of the mustard seed (Matt. 13:31-32), and the parable of the wheat and the tares (Matt. 13:24-30)—these are the most directly social of his teachings on the subject.

Four further parables shed enormous light on the Kingdom from the standpoint of the God-human dialogue; that is, what the Other—God—contributed, and what the human—I/you—must contribute. First, there is the parable of the workers in the vineyard (Matt. 20:1-16), who all received the same pay regardless of how long they had worked. The criterion for receiving the gift of the Kingdom is not the quantitative amount one has worked, but the qualitative state of willingness to work when called. In the parable of the feast (Luke 14:16-24), the great feast, the adapted, well-fed, and adjusted side does not respond, but the inferior, lost side of humanity and of ourselves responds. From the side of the Other there is plenty and abundance; from our side there is free choice to partake of it or not. Jesus said earlier, in effect, Blessed are the poor, those who weep, and those who hunger, for you have the most chance for the Kingdom. There is also the parable of the ten virgins (Matt. 25:1-12), five of whom had oil for their lamps, five of whom did not, and those who are ready respond when the door is opened at midnight and the bridegroom comes. Readiness, preparation, and alertness are requisites. Freedom of choice is again present—to move to a new level, or not to move. In both parables God is seen as potentially wrathful because of the lack of our response. He/She needs our response.

Finally, there is the parable of the Kingdom, where God forgives, but the one who is forgiven does not forgive his fellows. He allows the possibility of nonforgiveness by the one forgiven. The determining factor throughout again lies in the freedom of choice by the human in the midst of ambivalence. In Jesus' most radical statement, "The Kingdom of God is within you or within your midst" (Luke 17:21), lies the newest element: The birth of God in the psyche. This can be considered as a coming alive of Self as the image of God within human personality. This has been projected by his people into the messianic hope. This new birth for God and human was an archetypal movement of utmost significance. We need to explore what it came out of, where it has led, and where it has gone since his lifetime. The central moment of disclosure for him was the experience of the Baptism.

With what did Jesus as Jew come to the Baptism experience? He knew the God of Sinai, the Great I Am, as an emergent monotheistic reality. He knew that God as one of intentionality and of a restless longing for manifestation in history. He knew the covenant between God and human required obedience and alertness. He knew the God of the Hebrew Scripture as the God of Lamentations, "Is it not from the mouth of the Most High that good and evil come?" (Lam. 3:38), . . . and the God of Isaiah, "I form light and create darkness, I make weal and create woe, I am the Lord, who do all these things" (Isa. 45:7), . . . and of Deuteronomy, " . . . I wound and I heal . . . " (Deut. 32:39), and the God of Job, when Job said, " . . . Shall we receive good at the hand of God, and shall we not receive evil?" (Job 2:10).

Darkness as both unknown and evil was not split off as an autonomous element as in later Christianity: rather, Satan was part of God, offering choice in the midst of the ambiguities and ambivalences. This places a very different responsibility on humans. It is not to choose to go the way of goodness as opposed to evil, but rather to a way where one has to choose the best, the value, the will of God, in the midst of all the conflicting tendencies. The religious implications of this are enormous. Jesus also knew the hopes of his people for a Messiah, a Christ, a Savior, and an Anointed One of God who would establish a society, as Klausner says, "of political freedom, moral perfection, abundance in nature, fulfillment not only for the children of Israel, but for the whole human race." The vision of the Kingdom as a flowering, blossoming reality was held deeply by his people. Jesus knew the words and teachings of the long line of prophets before him, and placed himself in the line of those who preached the prophetic eschatology that the old world must die and a new one must come to birth through human effort; as opposed to an apocalyptic eschatology where the old world would be wiped out and a new one brought in by supernatural means. This, briefly, is Jesus' heritage, and it is absolutely vital for understanding Jesus as a person.

Now to return to the Baptism and the wilderness experience out of which the statement "the Kingdom of God is within you" (Luke 17:21) ultimately came. At that moment in time, the Holy Spirit descended from the transcendent God and entered into the psyche of the man Jesus of Nazareth. God now became immanent in a new way (even though there had been some movement toward it), but this God incarnated in Jesus was the God of opposites—both light and dark—as opposed to much of subsequent Christian thinking. It was always the concern of Jesus; and his teachings show that his was *not* a one-time or one-person incarnation, but an available reality for all others who would pay the price. This newness of the Holy Spirit within energized the Self into actuality. Because the Self had been projected by the Jews into the hope for a Messiah, Jesus was led to confront and reject the current forms, but not the reality behind them. This places the Self as an expression of God as the saving transformative element issuing within from the Holy Spirit. To this there was added by Jesus the concept of the Son of man from the Hebrew Scriptures not as messianic, but as a concrete existential expression of the Self at a conscious level.

Possibly the central achievement of Jesus was his non-identification with this hope for a Messiah. He never said "yes" or "no" when asked if he was the Messiah. Thus he felt the power of the Self was available to all, and more related to the Holy Spirit than to the Messiah or to the son. Many of you know the statement of Joachim de Flore, one of the great mystics of the eleventh century, who said, "the Old Testament was the Age of the Father, Christianity the Age of the Son, and now the new age would be the Age of the Holy Spirit." Until now, however, we in the Christian world have continued to project the Messiah, the only begotten son, onto Jesus. One might say that Jesus' Christology was one of absolute sureness of its reality in himself and in his teaching, and the conviction that others must find it in themselves. His own journey was one of coming to terms with the Will of God—outer/inner—and finding the saving element within, or finding within what God most truly intends for each of us to be. This is what it means to live our own myth as he lived his myth, and not to project the myth onto him. He lived life in such magnificence that it is no wonder people projected myth onto him during his lifetime and afterwards. But, in thus projecting, the power and the fullness of the inner archetypal possibility has been limited to doctrinal belief instead of being expressed in unique personal manifestation. This in no sense belittles the validity of the core of the Christian experience of the indwelling God, but we must examine its implications.

Dr. Jung has made a major contribution in pointing out that the Christian image of the Christ has excluded the dark and the feminine. I would like to go even a step further and raise some questions of what I think the study of the *Records* yields. Dr. Jung, in his desire to remain an empirical scientist, refused to write of the God whose image was reflected in the psyche. He saw the opposites, the tension, the movement within for wholeness, but further than that he did not go in his writings. For Jesus, what became alive in the Self is definitely a reflection of a God whom he served totally and whose nature is spelled out in Hebrew Scripture and throughout the *Records*. This God did include darkness and the feminine and, therefore, was more complete in His/Her incarnate form. The structure of God in the Self as seen in Jesus is for me more true to the facts of the psyche than that which has been put on him by Christianity. The desire, the intentionality behind the opposites for the new emergence of what I would call the third point, is clear and puts a demand on the person. It also gives support and help to the work of integration, which is to know the Self in this context. John had preached the opposites in God, as an outer split between good and bad people. At his Baptism, Jesus experienced these opposites coalescing and becoming reconciled within, as a work of the Holy Spirit that leads to a life of love. This experience lies behind all his teachings. This leads to a further question of whether we serve the Self, or serve the Christ within as an end in itself, or as part of a whole commitment to the total God. This has great implications for us within our Christian tradition, and also in the Jungian tradition.

Now to return to what was the new in Jesus. The richness of God without and within came to full bloom as did Jesus' compassion for the suffering of the wounded as part of God's suffering, the superb facing of evil and darkness in

God and in the world which led to his Cross. His deep sense of relationship between his inner resource and his outer action, his passionate concern that people choose life instead of destruction, thus affirmed the fact of freedom of choice and so much more.

What are the major distortions of Jesus' message that bring about the situation today of which Jeanne Hendrickse will speak? First, and foremost, we have put Jesus in the center—or Jesus Christ into the center—instead of God, thus worshiping him and losing the truer framework that the person Jesus and his potential hold for us. He was made equivalent to the Self, making it all good and great. The manifestations of the central Self were thereby limited, and the realities that Jesus lived—of death and rebirth, of virginal, continuous newness, of wound and healing—have become dogma and have become fixed on him as carrier.

Included in *C. G. Jung Letters, Vol. II* is a very critical letter to a minister, which is paraphrased here:

> We place ourselves under *his* cross, but by golly not under our own. The cross of Christ was *borne by himself* and was *his*. To put oneself under somebody else's cross, which has already been carried by him, is certainly easier than to carry your own cross amid the mockery and contempt of the world. That way you remain nicely ensconced in tradition and are praised as devout. Have your congregation understood that they must close their ears to the traditional teachings and go through the darknesses of their own souls and set aside everything in order to become that which every individual bears in himself as his individual task, and that no one can take this burden from him?

Jesus' life is a prototype of individuation and cannot be imitated. One can only live one's own life totally in the same way with all the consequence that entails.

Jung's letter describes what I think is the first major distortion of Christianity, and yet inevitably we need to understand it and go behind it. The second distortion, which grows out of the first, is that we have not been aware or cognizant of the nature of the totality of the psyche and of ourselves. The satanic element has become a powerful, negative, autonomous drive instead of being part of an original duality. Thus the power of personal evil and its ability to grow to autonomous, structured evil has not been faced or dealt with, and so we have the current world situation. The untouched shadow has grown large and ugly and into a cruel evil on a very large scale. This tragic unconsciousness drives us more and more towards a possible holocaust. By not dealing with ourselves in depth, we have projected onto others what really belongs to us. This again has great implications for global destruction.

Third, there is a distortion: We have laid the experience of the Holy Spirit onto the collective experience of Pentecost and have not worked with the deep, personal experience of Jesus at the Baptism, which led him to the encounter and conflict in the wilderness. The disciples after the crucifixion did not have a wilderness experience, and this made a decisive difference.

In conclusion, a total revision seems to me to be called for—a transformation of our understanding of the nature of Christianity, its values, and its inadequacies. It is no longer enough—although it is certainly needed—simply to have more religious people. It is no longer enough to work with the suffering and sadness of the world—even though, of course, that is extremely important today. Some of us must encounter the total impact of Christianity at its archetypal roots and make the simple, but profound and very difficult, shift from a religion *about* Jesus to the religion *of* Jesus. He lived his own inner myth to the fullest, and can enable us to live fully our own inner myths. Then we can help the world live to its fullest as well.

Jeanne Hendrickse: Elizabeth Howes has outlined her views of the Kingdom, what Jesus had to say about the Kingdom, the contributions of Jung on understanding the Self. I would like to focus on what Christianity did and did not do, which inititated us into the world we live in today. I would thus like to invite you to journey with me into the developing countries, and there encounter views of Christian history, oppression, liberation, revolution, transformation, freedom, and humanization.

As I prayed, read, and reflected in preparation for this evening, I became very much aware of splits, splits, splits. I had to stop and ask, Why? Why are these splits? Are these splits the result of our original splitting of the Tree of the Knowledge of Good and Evil? Is this splitting the basis of problems we face on our planet ecologically, socially, economically, spiritually, religiously? Does this splitting have to do with the violence, exploitation, dehumanization, and threat of nuclear holocaust we are encountering? What are the implications for the Kingdom, the rule of God? The Kingdom, the rule of God, is concerned not only with the personal, but with structures that come out of the personal; so we have to look at these structures of society. Western history is dotted with splits.

The Byzantine split in 453 C.E. resulted in the formation of the Eastern and Western Churches. Then came the Reformation and the split that resulted in the development of Western Protestantism. It is this split that ultimately resulted in the missionary movement of the nineteenth century, which mushroomed and then flourished in Africa, Asia, and Latin America. The missionary movement paved the way and became closely associated with colonialism, and later with imperialism and capitalism.

Do not get me wrong: I am not condemning Christianity per se. Eighty percent of our African people were educated in mission schools—I was too. I am, however, condemning the process of deculturalization and dehumanization that it brought. Christianity costs us much; Western theological authoritarianism provides a tremendous support for the status quo. Christianity, unfortunately, did not bring us the life and teachings of Jesus. What it brought was Western theological concepts and ideas and culture. It brought us Christianity dressed in Western garb. Salvation was thus the acceptance of Christ and Western ways.

Let us look briefly at the roots and evolution of oppression. The beginning of oppression in the so-called Third World countries has its roots in dualism. There is an innate duality and opposition in the nature of things; but somehow, because there was a refusal to deal with the opposites, hold them in dynamic tension, and work toward integrating them, the opposites became radically split apart from each other. As a result, duality becomes a system of dualism and splits. There seems to be a distinct split between we and they, the haves and the have-nots, both materially and spiritually.

The second step of oppression is the egocentric assumption of superiority versus inferiority, which leads to estrangement from the Source and humanity, and results in a spiderweb of conspiracy and violence. The dark and inferior side, which was not able to be accepted, is projected onto the dark and Third World nations. This, we see, has a direct bearing upon the culture of the people, specifically related to their language, their clothing, food, education, and what is often called their religion—their customs, traditions, myths, and beliefs. Missionaries were often unable to accept and deal with their own shadows. They did not understand the power and truth of the teachings of Jesus: Resist not evil. By resisting and denying their own evil, and projecting it, evil was given energy and power. The denial of personal evil, which was repressed, flared into the structural evil of racism and oppression. By denial of evil, evil was strengthened and fanned into flames that burned and destroyed cultures. Indigenous people were forced to learn the oppressor's language, for there was a need to communicate. Children at school were prohibited from speaking the vernacular. When they did, they were given a black punishment mark, and forced to do physical labor as a consequence. People were also forced by law to wear European clothes, for their nakedness was said to be a sin and abomination. Traditional names were changed to European Christian names, for the traditional name was unpronounceable, pagan, and meaningless. Pagan religion, myths, and beliefs were evil. So they had to forget them and become Christianized.

Raped of culture, the identity of the people became verbalized in terms of the oppressors, who called the oppressed people non-European, non-white, non-beings, non-humans. These are negating terms, for they define the oppressed people in terms of the oppressors. The oppressors are thus guilty of oppressing, but likewise the oppressed are guilty for allowing themselves to be oppressed. The oppressors are enslaved to the limitations of their own concepts of superiority and power, which stifles them into a vicious cycle of greed and self-annihilation. The oppressors need to be liberated from the need to care for the so-called underprivileged, deprived, and starving, and take care of their own inner starving, malnourished, deformed, dark children. The oppressed people do not need the handouts of fish from the First World; they need handups, so they can make their own fishing poles and catch their own fish. They need to become independent, self-sufficient humans. The First World needs to step back and step out of developing nations so that people in these lands will be able to stand on their own feet and walk their own way. Only when this happens will the oppressed people be able to step out of the "banking system" ways of thinking of the oppressors and develop their own value system. Only then will they be able to develop enough and produce enough to meet and fulfill their own needs—freedom, wholeness, and humanization.

This bondage to the law of least resistance is the bondage with which the First World Western capitalistic countries have enslaved the developing nations, which they call Third World as if they were third-class citizens. It enables the economically developed countries to exploit other countries, which they call underdeveloped. It enables the developed nations to steal the wealth of natural resources from developing nations and rape their land and people by planting coffee and rubber for export on their fertile lands, which are desperately needed for local food crops.

All three worlds need liberation, and liberation requires consciousness. All three worlds thus need to become conscious. The First and Second worlds need to be aware and conscious of the enslavement to their own egos. The threat of nuclear holocaust is very real, and they need to face the reality—to stop, listen, and reflect upon their present course of action, which leads towards self-annihilation and destruction of life on our planet Earth. They need to become conscious that we are dynamically interrelated and interdependent. Mutual respect and sharing is needed if we are to survive. It is therefore the task of the oppressed and exploited to liberate themselves, and in this process liberate their oppressors. Also the oppressors must let go of the destructive power and control.

The paradox is that it is only the power that springs from the weakness of the oppressed and exploited that is sufficiently strong to free both. This liberation cannot be achieved by chance, but only through the process of the oppressed people's quest for it. This fight, because of the purpose given it by the oppressed, constitutes an act of love opposing the lovelessness which lies at the heart of the oppressors' violence. Liberation must be submitted to the laws of the Kingdom.

Liberation is a painful childbirth. The one who emerges is a new creation, a new person, viable only as the oppressor-oppressed contradiction is superseded by the desire for humanization of all people. If this is not done, the oppressed becomes the oppressor. This new being is no longer the oppressed nor the oppressor, but humanity in the process of achieving freedom. The biblical emphasis on freedom means that one cannot allow another to define one's own existence. Human destiny is inseparable from a relationship with the Creator. When we deny our freedom or the freedom of others, we deny God. By responding to the *imago dei*, we cannot allow another to make us an "it." Affirming our freedom in God, we cannot obey laws of oppression. Thus, by disobeying oppressive laws, we say "yes" to God and "yes" to our own humanity as well as that of the oppressors.

The oppressors need to be liberated and freed from their desire to oppress and control. The oppressed need to be liberated and freed from thinking in terms of the oppressors. They must cease to want to achieve, to have homes, cars, and so on, for this is the value system of the oppressors. They must not take their focus away from their goal, which is freedom. Authentic freedom is grounded in the awareness of the universal finality of humanity and the agonizing responsibility of choosing between perplexing alternatives regarding existence. In the words of Dostoyevsky's grand inquistor—"freedom is a terrible gift." Freedom demands consciousness. Freedom demands conscious choice-making after weighing bitter alternatives. Freedom is standing at the center of the cross listening and choosing. It is solely by risking that freedom is obtained. For oppressed people, God is freedom. This symbol of freedom means wholeness. For oppressed people to see themselves as victims of oppression and injustice can lead to destructive fanaticism. On the contrary, when an oppressed individual can come to understand the historical process that has led to injustice, become conscious of the oppression, and take on responsibility for the oppression, the individual enters into a search for self-affirmation. This awakening of critical consciousness of the oppressive situation then leads the way to expression of social discontents.

Gustavo Gutierrez, an eminent Third World theologian, emphasizes three means of liberation, all of which are interdependent and comprise a single complex process: (1) The aspiration, the longing, and desire of oppressed people and social groups to escape the domination of wealthy countries and oppressive classes; (2) an understanding of history in which human beings assume conscious responsibility for their own destiny, leading to the creation of a new person and a qualitatively different society; and (3) the transformation of humans through encountering the life and teachings of Jesus the Savior (what we would call the saving element) who liberates humans from sin and estrangement—which is the ultimate root of all disruption of friendship and of all injustice and oppression. Oppressors need to know these teachings as well. The Kingdom of God provides the universal framework within which liberation of humans takes place. The oppressor cannot liberate me or my people; the revolutionary leader cannot liberate me, cannot liberate us.

It is important here to remember that, for example, in African creation myths, humans first exist in community. The community comes before the individual. An individual, however, who makes a choice—good or bad—has an impact and influence on the whole community. My individual choice thus affects community, for it is out of and as part of the community that I make my choice. Then there is the community itself that makes the choice; and as the people choose to be liberated, the process of liberation begins, for God is freedom. Authentic liberation is thus a process of humanization, a praxis that enables the oppressed to see, to know, to accept their oppression. As they become conscious of their oppression, they can choose to act and reflect upon their oppression in order to transform it. They can plan the action for the transformation of the oppression and the change of the oppressive situation in which they live. Liberation is thus not the solution or the end product. It is the means leading to humanization. The end product of liberation is humanization. Therefore liberation is not just from oppression, but liberation to be and become. And in this process of humanization, the situation of oppression is transformed. The solution is thus not simply to integrate the oppressed into the structures of oppression, but to transform the oppressive structures. In so doing, all can be humanized. The oppressed can thus become beings for themselves. Such transformation would obviously undermine the oppressive purposes where exploitation turns humans into automatons and does not allow people to think, plan, or strategize for themselves. Authentic liberation does not mean that we do not want adequate housing or enough food. Yes, it includes all of these, but the focus is humanization, for when humanization takes place, the need of those humanized would be consciously met.

What, then, is humanization, and when does it occur? Humanization takes place when I communicate and relate with another as a human with dignity and respect. When I can perceive the *imago dei* within my enemy and relate in an I-Thou manner (to use Buber's terminology). When we as Third World people speak about liberation, we do not mean liberation *from*, though liberation includes this. What we are talking about is liberation to be and become humanized, to be and become whole. We have problems with the concept of an omnipotent, omniscient God. It reminds us of the ever-present special branch of the South African police, always ready to act and imprison.

We grapple with the Christology of Western Europe. Their white Christ is inadequate for us. The most corrupting element was the wholly un-Biblical teaching that Christ dealt with other-worldly realities. One's reward would be in heaven. They taught us that if we had Jesus, then injustice, brutality, and suffering did not matter.

Jesus became a magical name, giving a distorted hope in a futuristic life in heaven. Thus, for many, Christianity became an opiate dulling the senses to the here and now on earth, calling for a focus of hope in the next life in heaven. The traditional eschatalogical suffering is interpreted as an entrance into heaven, for "blessed are they that have been persecuted for righteousness' sake; for theirs is the Kingdom of heaven" (Matt. 5:10). These are concepts which have stifled the oppressed and prevented them from standing on their own two legs, asking questions, and demanding the humanization I am talking about. They have been brainwashed into accepting their position—satisfied with their situation, for it is the will of God. The white Christ was and is irrelevant, because he was completely light—all darkness was excluded. Incarnation has to include both aspects to be meaningful.

As we study the *Records*, we see that at the Baptism the Holy Spirit descends into Jesus, bringing the Self to actualization in the psyche. Jesus faces this within himself, and is thus confronted by the messianic. By refusing the messianic role, Jesus faces the archetype behind the messianic, that which lies deep within the Self. Unfortunately, in Christianity the messianic was and is projected into the all-white, light Christ. This white-light Christ is not relevant or meaningful to oppressed people. He remains a Western stranger, whom others call us to serve. Black theology has now conceptualized the black Christ, who speaks more relevantly to the oppressed black people. The problem, however, still exists, for the messianic is still externalized in the black Christ.

Third World theologians are now searching for a meaningful Christology, and it is here that I see the real gift of the Guild methodology. Only when we withdraw our projections can something happen. We need to internalize and digest—that is, dialogue, reflect, and act upon Jesus' teaching. The Kingdom of God is within you. The Kingdom of God is amidst you—that is, the Kingdom is inner, but the Kingdom is also in outer situations. The apocalyptic view transforms evil and injustice into temporary good; black theology refuses to embrace a concept of God that makes the suffering of blacks the will of God. Likewise, contextual theology (or incarnational theology, as it is now called), refuses to embrace a concept of God that does not include freedom. Our hope is not wholly in the future. If we have only an eschatological hope for this world, we are paralyzed in the now. Our hope is here and now. But it is always still in the process of continuous becoming. As each individual chooses to do the will of God, the Kingdom is brought about. If people see themselves as oppressed and exploited, they conceive of themselves as less than human. They also realize the need for transformation of the oppressive situation.

The present capitalistic system of the West has and does oppress, exploit, and dehumanize Third World people; and therefore, in the process of their humanization, they have to plan their action, reflection, their praxis in transforming this dehumanizing, exploitative system into one in which they are humanized and can fully participate as humans. They have to keep their goal in focus. The goal is not liberation. The goal is transformation of the situation and humanization of all people. When this happens we have an example of the Kingdom of God coming, and still there is the mystery of the Kingdom. It is here and now and still always in the process of coming. This is the challenge to those of us who are concerned about the religious basis of the situation today.

Part II

Jeanne Hendrickse: This evening we invite you once again to journey with us to the developing nations, owners of the world's primary resources, yet called the Third World nations. Last week we discussed the background and causes of the problems we are encountering in our world today. We saw that mainstream Western European theology was irrelevant, and that the Third World people are in process of formulating their own theology. Tonight we will discuss the phases and evolution of Third World theology, leading to contextual liberation and incarnational theology. We will briefly look at the contribution of Gustavo Gutierrez, a Latin American theologian, and Paulo Freire, an educational pragmatist, and then we will focus on the value of the *Records* of the life and teaching of Jesus. Elizabeth Howes will then deal with the challenge to the First World from this situation.

The evolution of theology in developing nations seems to have gone through three phases. First, the apologetic period. During this phase, our people spent all their time just defining themselves, their thinking, and their theology, to fight First World theologians. The second phase was the period of adaptation during which our churches imitated and became carbon copies of the European light-white church. This church was irrelevant to the oppressed people in their situation of exploitation and suffering. They were denied the right to participate in history as subjects, and became dominated and alienated, the reasons for which I tried to explain in the previous lecture. In reaction to this second phase they then had to work on understanding the Bible out of their own context and situation of oppression and suffering. The Exodus remains the key to understanding God and themselves. The Decalogue is significantly prefaced: "I am the Lord your God, who brought you out of the land of Egypt, out of the house of bondage" (Exod. 20:2). God, the lawgiver, is seen essentially as God the liberator, God of freedom. Isaiah 62 is significant; in essence it reads, "Behold darkness shall cover the earth and thick darkness the people. But the lord will arise upon you and his glory will be seen upon you." Rightousness becomes a breastplate, a helmet of salvation.

Out of their oppression and suffering grew the third phase—contextualization—out of which contextual liberation and incarnational theology evolved. Contextual liberation theology enables the people to develop their own individual critical consciousness, which enables them to intervene and transform their world of oppression. They reflect on their situation, are challenged by it, and choose to act upon it to transform it. The people emerge from submission and submersion to intervention. Contextualization is a dynamic concept, for it is open to change and does not dictate outcome or solution in advance. Theology always takes place in a culture, and it is how the individual and collective confronts the word of God, or is confronted by the word. The word empowers them in their action and reflective process, as together they develop their praxis for liberation. Theology is thus contextualized or cultured in the context of the history of the people. It asks the question here and now, in this situation, How does the Kingdom express itself? What concrete instruments can be used in this context? Contextual theology is thus a situational theology, and critical analysis of the situation is essential.

Liberation theology. The term liberation arouses immediate suspicion, as it has a distinctive socialistic flavor with revolutionary overtones. Terms such as "oppressed" and "oppressors," and notions about what might be done to change their relationship, are abstractions until related to concrete situations. Gustavo Gutierrez, a South American theologian, offers a politicized theology, and he politicizes the idea of the Kingdom. The gift he brings is that he sees no split or dichotomy between spiritual and temporal salvation history and secular history. He feels that the Church has to take the side of the struggle, for it is static and devitalized, and not even strong enough to abandon the gospel. It is the gospel which is disowning the Church. The scope and gravity of the process of liberation is such that to ponder its significance is to examine the meaning of Christianity. The new society cannot yet be defined, and a just society is not the same thing as the Kingdom.

Paulo Freire sees the vocation of humanity to be the development of the individual person as a subject that can act upon the world, bringing about a fuller, more meaningful, and richer life, both individually and collectively. He stresses the importance of joining subjectivity and objectivity. The process of liberation cannot employ methods of dehumanization, and thus dialogue and liberating education become essential. The *word* is important, for silence can be a sign of oppression. The word "liberation" contains two dimensions: reflection and action. They are dynamically interrelated, and if one is sacrificed, the other suffers; this can then lead to verbalism or activism. True word is therefore seen as praxis.

The word is thus the right of all, and not the privilege of a selected few. Those who have been denied their primordial right to speak by the negative Christ image that we saw in the last lecture must reclaim that right, and in so doing eliminate and transform dehumanizing aggression. Here I see implications from the *Records*. For Jesus teaches that it is what comes out of the heart that defiles— that is, the word—and not that which is taken into the mouth. Dialogue is important in the liberating process, for when there is true dialogue, there is an I-Thou encounter, a humanization occurs. By humanization I mean becoming completely and totally human. There can be no dialogue without love, humility, faith in humanity, and in the individual's power to remake and recreate. Hopelessness is silence, and denies and flees from evil, thus giving it power; while dialogue confronts evil. Dialogue requires critical thinking and thus generates critical thinking. We cannot have an authentic liberation theology until the oppressed can freely and creatively express themselves in society and church, or until they are the artisans of their own liberation. Liberation must be submitted to the laws of the Kingdom.

Incarnational theology is liberating the gospel from Western trappings in order that the truth which Jesus of Nazareth reveals about God may encounter the spiritual, cultural, and intellectual worlds of the Third World people. Issues of moratorium center on selfhood and self-reliance. They deal with our capacity to contribute significantly to the humanization of the world and are dependent on our rediscovery and redefining of our own identity. The incarnation in Jesus of the dark and the light can be recaptured and lived by others. The incarnation of the Holy Spirit did not stop with Jesus. Incarnation continues to happen. The value of contextual liberation, black, Third World theology, is that the center is Christ, the saving element. The problem, however, is that the Christ is either all white, all light, or all black. There is no opposite held in dynamic tension in the Christian Christ. The saving element is still being projected and externalized in Jesus Christ, and does not express the true values of the Self within. An African theologian, Gabriel Setluone, grapples with Christology, and asks: Who is Jesus? How does he become the supreme human manifestation of the divinity? As the Messiah of Judaism, and the Christos of Hellenistic Christianity? What does Messiah or Christos mean in the African context?

Here is where I see the real value of the *Records*. For what is needed is the dynamics of the *Records* of the life and teachings of Jesus, which I see as an incarnational theology, bringing the *saving element into the Self*. The dynamic contributions of the *Records* will now briefly be looked at.

The first contribution is the laws of the Kingdom, the Shamah: Love God with all your heart, mind, soul, strength. Next we need to find the instruments, the tools of the Kingdom. An important basic and relevant teaching of Jesus is this: resist not evil. When we look at the reality of the destructive power and evil of corporations, we need to accept this evil, look it in the eye, reflect to see where God is operative and moving, then confront this evil with the tools of the Kingdom. We need to seek the will of God, listen, dialogue, reflect over and over, then act according to the laws of the Kingdom. Evil pulsating with life has many tentacles, like an octopus. Chopping off a tentacle using instruments of destruction and evil do not help. We need to go to the head, the central force, the powerhouse, the structures of organization and control, which hold and supports the tentacles: for only when this happens can transformation happen.

We need to continuously remind ourselves of patience. Patience is an important ingredient of the Kingdom, for the Kingdom grows very slowly, but it does grow, under the very eyes of the oppressors. It grows and does so in darkness. The seed of the Kingdom, once planted, needs to be nourished. It needs to be analyzed as to what nutrients are needed. This is done by reflection, dialogue, and analysis, always keeping in centrality the Kingdom, the laws and the tools of the Kingdom. Personally, I have problems with violence. In the past I have spoken very strongly about Newton's laws of physics: For every action, there is an equal and opposite reaction. So if the action is violent, the reaction must be violent. Fight fire with fire. Natural laws of physics, yes. What do the natural laws of the Kingdom say? Love God with all, and neighbor as self. It is easy to stand here and say this in a First World country to a basically white audience; but out there in the struggle, when one watches one's young men tortured and unborn babies shot in their mothers' wombs, it is hard. Hatred fills our beings, and we want to destroy and kill, giving power to evil and destruction. Does God need this? The wrath of God that could destroy the planet with a wink of an eye? This very God that could pray to Him/Herself, may it be my will that my mercy and love overcome my wrath. No, this God does not need our wrath. This God needs our mercy, our forgiveness, our love. This God needs our transformed wrath: That third point in which wrath is included, that is, the wrath that had been transformed. How do we deal with the situation? I have no answer. I struggle as each of us struggles; but I believe that as the insignificant I, the Self, faces evil, something happens to the evil in the universe. Something happens to the darkness within God. Jesus' teaching on the single eye, the focused eye, and that the light be not darkness, says something.

We are reminded and must remember that the Kingdom grows slowly. Pregnantly, we in the Third World wait expecting birth any moment. Birth cannot be forced. When the baby is ready, the birth takes place, the child is born. We are demanding the birth of our child, humanization. We are demanding dialogue. We are demanding change and are working toward the fulfillment of transformation of the situation. But constantly we need to do this within a reflective context, listening to the operative God within the situation. Childbirth is painful. Sometimes the mother dies giving birth, giving life to the new creation that emerges out of destruction and suffering. Jesus continues his dialogue with God and self. He submitted his own will to the demands and needs and requirements of the Will of God. Jesus was crucified, but it is in this very Crucifixion that Jesus and God are set free. Liberated. God is freedom. Human is freed. Jesus is humanized. God is humanized. The Kingdom comes for Jesus, for God, for humanity. And yet the Kingdom continues to come today as we constantly

work in God's vineyard, Earth. Our wages are equal. They
are the same. The wage is humanization. Freedom. Wholeness. That is salvation for God, salvation for humanity.

The question was asked, How can I become Third
World when I live in the First World? To be Third World
means your heart, your soul, your mind, your body are
where the dispossessed are. Being reconciled to God,
humanity, and nature is what is important. The real question is: Where is your identity? Where is your being? Does
it lie with the oppressed or with the oppressors? Sinful
humanity too can be declared righteous. The black revolution in America meant death of America as it was during
slavery. Likewise, a change within the Church needs to
take place. There is the required and needed death. The old
Church and old Church structures of power and control
that used instruments of evil must die, and a new birth is
needed. The Church must decide where its identity lies.
Will it continue to cater to forces of oppression, or will it
embrace the causes of liberation, humanization, freedom,
and wholeness for all of humanity, and not cater to the
status quo?

Let me give you an example. One of the largest Protestant denominations in the United States had their pension
funds invested in South Africa. We talked with these people. They said that they were with us, but that they had to
take care of themselves when they retired. Where is the
priority of the Church, the church leaders? I am with you,
but I must see to my own needs. Is this a fake understanding of self interest, one which is ego-bound in its intentions? We need to put our lives together. We cannot split
our thinking from our doing. Thought and action must co-
incide. We must be at one with ourselves, with our neigh-
bors, and thus with God. This is what atonement is: Atonement with all. There can be no dualism, no split.

Let's look at what impedes the Kingdom of God, and
look at ways to inaugurate the Kingdom, the rule of God.
Sin impedes the Kingdom. Sin separates and alienates us
from God, humanity, ourselves. By submitting myself to
the Will, my confrontation for this one space can be the
beginning of confrontation in other areas of darkness. All
of us working together toward the coming inauguration of

the Kingdom bring about its inauguration. The Kingdom has already been inaugurated. It is here and now, a seed growing slowly. Yet the inauguration takes place daily, as each committed to doing the Will reflects and takes action according to the Will.

We, however, cannot look at human life as individuals only. We have to look at the structures of society, for the Kingdom is ultimately concerned with structures. The arrangement of human society either inaugurates or impedes the Kingdom. Individuals may do one thing that is according to the Kingdom; but unless their activity, their action, has an impact on the structure, it is of no avail. For Christians it may be tremendous to be saved, and maybe for them being saved means the Kingdom does come. Their souls are received by God when they die. This is wonderful. But how does their being saved affect the structure? How can being saved transform structures? The Kingdom in its ultimate shape is global. It is the holy structure of the whole universe of human life. The question is: Has my, has your, has our being saved had an impact on the whole scene? And what impact has it had? Has it helped in the transformation of the situation?

The Kingdom is the plan of God for a world which is a family. We the people are God's universal family, and thus we have to follow the Will. God's family is required to work in the vineyard of the universe. How, then, do God and God's family work? The laws of the Kingdom are central. Love God with all, and love neighbor as self. God's intended family is thus built with humans who choose to love. Love is thus a prerequisite for the Kingdom. The promotion of relationships is dictated by love. Love is the mutual concern of God's family. Mutual responsibility and respect for each other is essential, for this is what the Kingdom needs. It is when people go out of themselves, break out of egocentric patterns and self-centered interests that they see how worthless they are unless connected and interrelated with the interests of others. When this happens, relationships widen and the Kingdom is facilitated. When I am working, saying I want to receive the Kingdom within myself, so it can begin to grow, I am trying to assimilate, to receive God, the spirit of Love. When infused

by the Holy Spirit, all my ways of acting—attitudes, relationships, investments, and so on—would be infused with
the Holy Spirit. I would try to help others to do the same.
This is loving neighbor as self. As brothers and sisters,
children of God, we would love each other, and be concerned with one another. We thus would challenge the
whole situation.

Too often, in most arenas of life it is self-interest and
egoism that dominate and create the mentality of survival
of the fittest. This to me is the basis of capitalism. We ask:
Can capitalism be Christianized? No it cannot be. It cannot
become all light, all white, all good, but it can be transformed. It has to be if we are to survive. Capitalism is based
on self-interest at the expense of exploiting others. If we
take self-interest away, we no longer have capitalism.
Christianity has failed because it has been trying to Chris-
tianize capitalism. Capitalism for the Church in the name
of the Church—this is self-interest, this is building on sin,
on estrangement, and separation. The coming of the Kingdom is based on one law, the law of the Kingdom (Luke
10:25-28).

When I am imbued with the Kingdom, I start to live the
Kingdom; where I go I challenge what goes against the will
and against the sons and daughters of the Kingdom. Anything against this law is not the Kingdom. The questions
we have to ask ourselves are: What impedes the Kingdom?
What inaugurates the Kingdom? By this action, by this
choice, am I impeding or am I inaugurating the Kingdom,
the rule of God? As I struggle to kill the old one within me, I
struggle and thus join others in the struggle, and in so doing form a wider circle. Those imbued with the Kingdom
can then form networks to strengthen each other, for the
Kingdom is within and among you. Coalitions of people
with the same preoccupation supporting and strengthen-
ing each other can be formed like a circle of dots. As we
come closer and closer to each other, we also move closer
and closer to the center. And as we move closer and closer
to the core, the Source, we move closer and closer to each
other. This to me is an example of inaugurating the Kingdom, the rule of God.

Elizabeth Howes: What crucial learning can we receive from what Jeanne Hendrickse has brought? How does this learning affect our own journey and its relation to the world? And how we can help to bring about a new Kingdom of meaning if we survive the threat of nuclear destruction?

Reflection and action are two key words needed for the practice of transformation, because only through them are we led to objectivity in the fullest sense of the word. After the Baptism experience, the Holy Spirit led Jesus to the wilderness for deep confrontation. His reflection on the interaction of struggle with tension outwardly led to action of perception, clarity, and wisdom. From this experience we can learn much about the critical analysis that is needed for creative action. I should like to consider three areas where reflection is demanded in us, and to suggest an image for their solution.

First, we must face, individually, where we stand in reference to dealing with the oppressed and the oppressor in our society. We of the First World must know whether our fundamental alliance is with oppressor or oppressed. This is the religious task of knowing how we see God operating in existential patterns. What is His/Her will? As was pointed out in the last lecture, we all stand in guilt by allowing a system of exploitation backed by Christianity to produce the situation it has. Our identity must be clarified in ourselves—not sentimentally, but by knowing ourselves consciously and inwardly. We must know our own projections behind our social attitudes. With what groups do we identify, and what groups do we reject? For instance, our sympathy for certain groups may come from the undealt-with archetypal realities within us (i.e., many liberals stand with minority or rejected groups because of their own repressed minority side). This does not make for a very stable social concern. All this takes an objectivity made possible only through religious depth and analysis in order that we might discover the truth within us, and watch our reaction to outer situations—not what we intend, but what we *do*.

How can we live in the First World and be with the Third World? It requires the inner searching of our own selves and outwardly knowing why we are doing what we are doing and what we are supporting. I take this to be an absolutely fundamental problem out of Jeanne Hendrickse's presentation to us, because it is so easy to be glib, it is so easy to be sentimental, it is so easy to be hypocritical.

Second, we need with ruthless honesty and compassion to know individually where we stand; and where the Church stands, if we are part of a Church in regard to the Christ-image, because of its influence in Christianity and particularly in the Third World. In the last lecture we went into this in some detail, but it may not hurt to clarify it a bit further. Each one of us needs to ask, "Am I still accepting a Christ-image that is all light, with darkness cut off? Am I still letting Jesus and some messianic hope carry my journey?" Insofar as I remain unconscious of my answer to this, I contribute to the spirit of the negative side of Christianity. Insofar as I work to carry my own journey as an individual and in community, I permit the fine light of the laser beam of the true Self to penetrate the shadows of the world. This means thinking and reflection on my religious process and the choices I am living by. We saw last week how the core of what has been taken to the Third World countries has been a light, Savior Christ image very far from Jesus' own attitude. Perhaps as one person said afterwards, we need to stop preaching Jesus Christ and start preaching the Holy Spirit—not in the charismatic sense, but as seen in the wilderness experience of Jesus as the thrust of God in the psyche towards genuine consciousness. This personal searching must carry over to willingness to challenge within the Church, when it is appropriate, whether it is as minister, priest, or parishioner. This takes courage, but courage we must have to get behind the whole messianic Christ issue to its archetypal roots so it can truly function as the image of God within or as the Self helping the integrative progress of the Kingdom. This Self must be free from both its Judaic and Christian forms to develop, to flower, to blossom, and to become the basis for a true community of brotherhood and sisterhood.

Ira Progoff has made the interesting statement that Jung's psychology, which seems to be so individual, is at the same time the only psychology that really has a religious basis of community, because the idea of the Self is not only individual, but also is universal in community. From this Self, if we can get at it, we can let ourselves be motivated by the compassion that is part of the Self in its appropriate setting. For instance, it is hard to know when to give and when not to give; when to respond overtly and when not to respond overtly. We can learn to open ourselves to the suffering of others if the Self is freed. We can be both involved and attached, and that we do need to be. We can learn to dialogue with people without needing to win, yet without hiding our convictions. Dialogue assumes listening as well as talking. We can grow in courage to challenge collective situations breaking through the tight shell of controlled manipulation and domination. These steps, and so much more, would perhaps slowly tear out the weeds and plant new seeds of the word that would truly become incarnated in flesh. They are suggestions of how acting from the image inside that which Jesus lived, of all-inclusiveness, would differ from acting—however well meaning—out of the image of Christ or Savior as a light-sided masculine reality.

Third, intrinsic in what has been said is the analysis and confrontation of the problem of evil, as Jeanne Hendrickse has so eloquently pointed out. Evil repressed, rejected, neglected, projected is, to a large extent our Christian image. We have not wanted to look at the social implications of the structures of evil and exploitation; we have not wanted to see how they are the outgrowth and extension of our personal evil. Jesus' approach, one might say, his methodology of dealing with evil, is found in "resist not evil" as part of doing the Will of God.

This phrase, "resist not evil," needs explanation. God was operative for Jesus in all situations offering choice and discrimination. Remember, Jesus said, "Sufficient unto the day is the evil thereof" (Matt. 6:34). What does resist not him that is evil mean (Matt. 5:39)? It does *not* mean repressing evil and pretending it isn't there, it does *not* mean turning our eyes from it, it does *not* mean returning evil with evil, it does *not* mean projecting it all outside. It *does* mean looking at it, seeing it, understanding its divine *and* human root as a reality, and in each situation to see what can be done with it to transform it. It can only be changed by its frank acknowledgment and by bearing the guilt of being part of it. In this way, slowly, humanized beings come to be, and social structures perhaps can be changed. Big transformations can come from small steps if we discover where we stand, where our own identities detach from collective labels, and where our own inner word of truth really wants to lead us. Jesus resisted not evil by his decision to do the Will of God until the very end.

This leads me to my final consideration. What images can most help us to change these instruments of destruction, hate, and fear into the instruments of creativity and love? Perhaps one is the Cross if understood differently from the orthodox interpretation. If we reflect objectively on what the cross meant to Jesus we may find some way for transformation in ourselves. In Gethsemane, Jesus chose to let himself be arrested, go to trial, be killed by enemies because he was seeing an all-inclusive God of light and dark, masculine and feminine, wanting reconciliation. At that point, he becomes a redeemer of God, not saved by God. He was at the center of the Cross, as each of us can be. His active transformation helped to transform the wrath of God to the love of God. This perhaps was the final fruit of eating of the Tree of the Knowledge of Good and Evil. Having eaten that fruit so profoundly all his life, he was now at the final manifestation.

In closing, I would like to say that as a First World person I feel we have only barely touched the implications of contextual theology—that is, seeing things within historical incarnational theology actually incarnating in ourselves, rather than simply believing in dogma. What could be the implications of these for us, from the study of the *Records*, and for restructuring Christianity, or perhaps moving beyond Christianity? These are the things I feel deeply about. In a renewed challenge and willingness to search for my own real identity in the sight of God and, I hope, for you to search for yours, to become more ready to serve the demands of the Kingdom, outer and inner, to find a love more total than we have known, to be part of the process of moving the planet from possible destruction to

possible humanization may be the validation of why I was
born.

Mythic Truth, Historical Truth, and Religious Consciousness

All events in this nuclear age, inner and outer, point to the need for increased religious and psychological consciousness for ourselves and for society. Today there is a need for new symbols of meaning or revitalization of old symbols in our Judaic-Christian religious concepts on which, consciously or unconsciously, our lives have been and are built. This is the need to get at the core of archetypal meaning within the symbol in a deeper way, so that our lives can be transformed into much more living, vibrant realities. This process will lead us to deal with the confusion of myth and history in Christianity, which has conditioned our lives and therefore the relation of myth and history in ourselves.

Fundamentally, *we have mythologized the historical man, Jesus, and we have historicized the mythic structures on which he lived.* To understand this and its total implications, myth and history must be briefly defined.

In each of us there is a deep reservoir of inner images and meanings—the interior world—which is the source of art, of creative scientific insight, of the dreams of humanity, of religious visions and experiences. These inner presences Dr. Jung has called the archetypes. The meanings of this inner individual world are expressed in the great myths of all periods of history. Immediately, this shows us that myths are in no way lies or unreality. They are truths that have evolved out of these archetypal meanings. They have been formulated by people who put trust in their inner vision and imaginings. Such are the myths of creation

* Presented at First Unitarian Church, San Francisco, California, under the auspices of the Guild for Psychological Studies, April 9, 1984.

known in the Greek, Egyptian, and Native American myths, as well as in the Genesis myth of the Hebraic Scriptures—they are all manifestations of God's activity in the human soul. This reservoir is in each of us, and our creative relationship to it is essential. If it is blocked, neglected, or pushed down, the result is some form of disease. Mythic truth, then, lies within us as a source of vitality. What has happened to this archetypal depth in Christianity is what concerns us.

History, on the other hand, refers to social and individual forces in the outer world, as well as in the inner world, that condition our lives. If we are related to our inner mythic realities and also hold a good relation to the outer pressures of history, we can work to find the purpose of both of them, no matter how difficult they are at times. If we are not related to this inner realm, we are tossed about and become distorted by the historical events. The creative challenge to our conscious side—what we know as our ego—is to relate as fully as possible to this inner world, to honor its content, and relate it to the existential moment of history. Thus inner and outer can come into harmony, and this forms the basis of a true religious psychological consciousness.

Today, a frightening lack of consciousness and integration has resulted in the symptoms of violence and cruelty we know so very well around us. It is no longer enough, to my mind, to be more sincere, more serious, more dedicated to the truth that we ultimately serve. Some new freshness of approach is needed, and perhaps today it is possible for two reasons: One, the way of studying the Gospels that I have been involved with these many years, attempts to disentangle the confusion. Two, the knowledge from analytical psychology, which gives us new tools to understand the anatomy of religious experience.

What is the basis of Christianity? Christianity is founded on the mythologizing of the history of the man, Jesus. The human person, Jesus, became identified, partly during his lifetime but mostly after his death, with all the major mythic motifs that for centuries have attached to hero figures. It often is said that Christianity is a historical religion. This, along with the mythologizing, has deprived us of any picture of him in his own struggle for identity, personhood, and consciousness. He is believed to have incarnated the myths by his identification with them, thereby bringing them into a new substantial reality in his living. From the Baptism onward—or perhaps really beginning with the Virgin Birth account—through his life, to the Crucifixion, and through it to the Resurrection accounts, Jesus is portrayed in the image of this hero myth. This is central to our understanding, because our individual archetypal grooves and our own patterns have been conditioned deeply by these events.

History becoming mythologized has been, then, the basis of our religious belief. This necessary confusion has held tremendous value for two thousand years, with great positive results. Without this identification to carry the archetype, we would not be sitting here tonight. The art, the liturgy, the sacramental, and many other aspects of Christianity have all been enormously rich. But there have also been great limitations. These limitations have included the emphasis on perfection rather than on wholeness; a lack of inclusion of darkness and evil; a feeling of being protected by the God image, rather than being urged to take more responsibility for our own actions and relations to our personal divine forces. It has also failed to emphasize the feminine.

Not all of the elements in the psyche that have been newly discovered through analytical psychology have yet found their way into the Christian myth. The Christian myth has also not included the dialogic relationship from Jesus' Jewish heritage of his I-Thou relationship with his God. Rather, it has been replaced by a belief in him, Jesus (Christ), who would do all good things for us. Too many psychic splits have been left untouched, and this contributes vastly to the decadent social situation in which we find ourselves today.

The other side of mythologizing history has been to historicize mythic realities. Now what does this mean, the historicizing of mythic reality? The great myths as expressions of the Self are death/rebirth, wounded healer, birthing from the virginal, and the messianic Christ saving element. They have been concretized—made literal—through the projection of their dynamic content onto the one person, Jesus. Yes, these myths did achieve a substantial reality due to the projection onto this one person, but they became completely colored by their Christian clothes. The Christian interpretation of these mythic archetypes received the devotion of those who believed in the dogma, and on the whole they also responded to the central figure as a supernatural figure. But the deeper and more significant point needs to be understood: Not only did the myths lose their unique possibility of fulfillment outside the Christian form, but it has not been seen that Jesus himself *lived* these mythic truths, thereby adding a different dimension to them. I repeat: Jesus himself lived these mythic truths, which are the ones that have mainly been projected onto him.

This changes the picture of both of them and of him. The mythic truths lived and manifested in him yield a dynamic picture of fruits and of outcomes. He himself becomes a different kind of person for us, a different figure. He's there, but new. His personal history based on his relationship to God transcendant, situational, immanent, could be seen in his living and teaching. Behind everything he did and said, the immanent God as Source inside him was there. It provided a well of knowing and of wisdom, and his creative "I" met it in dynamic confrontation.

This approach—seeing him with his myth—may well meet the demands of our unconscious, which today often rebels against the limitation of belief and wants a deeper religious root. In this way we may find within our own Western tradition new archetypal meaning that has been carried by Christianity, but was actually lived by Jesus and is transmittable to us. We can see that in historicizing the myth, we not only put the myth in Christian form, but we lose the value of seeing the myth lived by Jesus, and lose the chance to hear his teaching which in essence is continually contained in this form: Live your own reality and myth—don't put it on me. I feel with Dr. Jung that we may gain great value and insight from the East, but we must recognize that we are Western in our psychic structure, and we need to find our fundamental roots within the Western tradition.

Now let us turn for a moment to the outstanding places where the truth he lived has become historicized. Perhaps these can be redeemed out of the structure and made more available to us if we dig deeply. First, from the Baptism experience onward, Jesus lived as a son born from the descent of the Holy Spirit within his human substance. This experience translates into how the Holy Spirit constantly impregnates substance and leads to new birthing or to a masculine-feminine *conjunctio*. One particular statement by Jesus, " . . . the Holy Spirit shall tell you in that very hour what ye ought to say . . . " (Luke 12:12) is an example, perhaps of the virginal . . . of the acceptance of something virginal that can happen in the moment. This was for him a dynamic experience, one of the roots of his living. And later, when he was made into the Son, his experiences concretized into the myth of the Annunciation and of the Virgin Birth. He related to the son archetype, and said we could do the same. But he, of course, became it in the doctrine of "the only begotten Son."

Second, for Jesus the death/rebirth motif, which was universal in Greek and Egyptian mythic tradition, was enunciated in his great teachings of selling all for the pearl, losing life to save it, the parable of the prodigal son, and in many other places. It was lived by him in his whole journey—including opposites, facing dark and light, being all-inclusive in his attitude with the utmost courage. Later, of course, the myth of death and rebirth takes the form of belief in Jesus' physical Resurrection. This is what I feel that he lived. It is available to us if we will respond to it, and if we are willing to take it out of the form in which it has been held as doctrine for these two thousand years.

Third, the gospel accounts are full of healings where Jesus is portrayed as doing the healing. He then becomes the mythic wounded healer. In reality, he was careful on many occasions to point out that it was not he who did the healing; rather, it occurred because something of a symbolic nature, some symbol of wholeness and healing, was aroused in the person by Jesus. Jesus was a catalyst, and healing was aroused because he related to it and aroused it in other people, but he himself did not do the healing. Each of these instances can help us to see the disentangling of the confusion of myth and history, and the new realignment of it. Seeing Jesus' own relation to myth and how he brought it into his history leads to new possibilities for us if we will search for his *way*, and not just for him.

One more instance, the most central and difficult to describe, is Jesus' relationship to the messianic-Christ image of his people. From the wilderness on, he never answered "yes" or "no" to questions put to him about messiahship. He never refused it, and he never accepted it. He left the question with the questioner. Thus we are left with the struggle of our evaluation of his answer and of our own answer in ourselves to this central question of the saving element inside us behind the longing for the savior.

All theological statements have mythology behind them. Take the phrase "the only begotten Son, the one-time incarnation." Beginning with the Baptism, of which I have just spoken, Jesus felt himself the beloved Son, a phrase we find over and over again in Hebrew Scripture. He stressed the achievement of life and sonhood (or daughterhood, if you will) by a choiceful act of commitment. Anyone could become a beloved child. Anyone could work at the problem of incarnating the value of God.

Take the phrase, "The Lamb of God who taketh away the sins of the world." I read in the Gospels a continual stress by Jesus of the necessity of individual responsibility for sin, of the continual presence of evil to be accepted as part of the whole.

I would like to read part of a letter from Dr. Jung to a minister. Dr. Jung used the term "Christ" in speaking of Jesus because he did not make a distinction between the two as I would. Dr. Jung writes: Christ forces man into the impossible conflict. But we imitate Christ and hope he will deliver us from our own fate. Instead of bearing ourselves, i.e., our own cross ourselves, we load Christ with our unsolved conflict. We place ourselves under his cross, but by golly, not under our own. Have your congregation understood that they must close their ears to traditional teaching and go through the darkness of their own souls and set aside everything in order, to become that which every individual bears in himself as his individual task, and that no-one can take this burden from him?

I think that speaks for itself and needs no addition from me. It is one of the many places in Jung's wonderful two-volume collection of his letters, where he particularly addresses himself to the religious field and to ministers.

The untangling of Jesus' relationship to the messianic also offers a solution to the split between the Jesus of history and the Christ of faith. The new historical Jesus that could emerge from this approach would be one that includes his relationship to the Christ inside and leaves us to find our own expression. There would be no split between the historical Jesus and the Christ of faith; rather, the new historical Jesus would include his relationship to the Christ.

The figure of Jesus in this new approach contains a great numinosity, different from the Christian picture in all its forms, but moving each of us to take responsibility for our own lives. The revisioning and reinterpretation will take work, conceptually and personally, to dig out in the human psyche what is within Christian projection so that we may live the truth more completely. It requires openness and flexibility to move into sacred precincts of rigidly held beliefs. Only the possible fruit spurs us on, the fruit of bringing our own history and mythic depths together into wholeness for our sake and for the sake of society, and perhaps for the sake of God. And another, outer fruit might be our moving toward more dialogue with people of other religions, most especially what is called the Christian-Jewish dialogue.

In conclusion, then, these are the questions I would like to put to you—the kind of questions that have absorbed me through these many years, and which absorb me now. Would it not be a paradox if Jesus, who was pre-Christian, turned out to be truly post-Christian in the new age? What would happen in our world if we each lived our own myths in our own historical setting? What would happen to the great myths themselves if, freed from dogma and creed, we responded to them as if they contained the archetypal reality that could be the basis of our own lives? What would happen if we saw Jesus as bringing a new mutation in the evolutionary scheme of the Western world?

Moses' experiences of the burning bush and the Great I AM of Sinai were certainly central evolutionary moves. Is it possible that Jesus takes those experiences even one step further? Finally, could the mythologizing of history and the historicizing of myth change into the possibility of a new creation, wherein mythic truth and historical truth come together in our own lives and in the ongoing creativity of the religious process?

Descent-Ascent:

The Journey of the Holy Spirit

It blows where it wills; it moves across darkness; it is a still small voice; it is a fire; it is breath, wind, a dove; it is Sophia; it is communication of and from God. Dr. Jung wrote that the God-image of the Holy Spirit has a nature that unites the opposites. It is mute, eternal, unfathomable, in whom God's love and God's terribleness come together in wordless union. Its function is thus a reconciling one between all opposites. It is this aspect of the Holy Spirit as reconciling that I want to explore, for it seems to me the central religious problem. Jung says elsewhere that the problem is no longer just between God and human, but between opposites within the God-image.

Many of you know of Joachim de Flora, an Italian mystic (c. 1132-1202), who made the assertion that Judaism was dominated by the Father image, Christianity by the Son image, and that the new age would be dominated by the Holy Spirit. The movements today that center on the Holy Spirit may be one indication that the new age, the Aquarian Age, is in fact starting, is now in process of being born; and an understanding of its nature is imperative. This new age comes at a time when the Son image of Christianity—the Christ image—is undergoing tremendous change. The Holy Spirit movement indicates new movement in the inner archetypal world and of unconscious forces; much is stirring there. It is because of my deep respect for these movements that I feel some further exploration of them is needed. The Holy Spirit can be a

* *Presented at the First Unitarian Church, San Francisco, California, May 12, 1978, under the auspices of the Guild for Psychological Studies.*

vital force for the development of consciousness today through the integration of opposites, or it can degenerate into pseudo-spirituality, inflation, and self-righteousness. Because we are speaking of the divine, inner and outer, so we must deal with it gently, passionately, urgently—not only with our hearts and minds, but with the core of ourselves.

This mysterious, functioning Holy Spirit cannot be explored without seeing it in relationship to its historical roots in the Hebrew Scriptures. The task, then, is first to see the background out of which Jesus emerged and to examine his relationship to the Holy Spirit, and then to speak, very briefly, to the post-synoptic account of the Holy Spirit in the later Christian writings. As we do this we must constantly keep in mind the distinction between what Jesus has to say and offer, and what developed later in Christianity. These are the central questions we will be watching for. What is the relationship of the Holy Spirit to the problem of darkness and Satan? What is the relation of the Spirit to its opposite, Substance? Does it come into matter or does it emerge out of matter, or both? What is the relationship of the Spirit to the function of the ego—that is, the conscious I of the personality? What are the differences between the working of the Holy Spirit in an individual and in a group or multitude of people? What is the cost of letting oneself be moved by the Holy Spirit and becoming conscious of it rather than remaining ignorant of it or being dominated by it? And finally, what is the relation of the Holy Spirit to the messianic Christ image, and how do both of them relate to the concept of the Self in Jung's sense?

Let us start, then, with the creation myth in our Judaic-Christian tradition. Here is the account in Genesis:

> "In the beginning . . . the earth was without form and void, and darkness was upon the face of the deep; and the Spirit of God was moving over the face of the waters." (Gen. 1:1-2)

Here, in the beginning, we have Yahweh (God), wind, breath, as an energizing thrust over formlessness. "Let there be light," he said. Let there be patterning, let potential arise from within the formlessness. What else is there in the beginning of Genesis? There is the creation of male and female: "So God created man in his own image, in the image of God he created him; male and female he created them" (Gen. 1:27); the two opposites, masculine and feminine, male and female. There is the statement of bipolarity: the knowledge of good and evil. There is Yahweh and the serpent within God, presenting the bivalence of God. There is the expulsion from the Garden. I cannot take time to go into the whole story, but must trust your memory of it. There is the expulsion; there is the suffering; there is the flaming sword placed at the gate of the Garden, which one would have to go through or touch or do something with, to guard the way back to the Tree of Life. Here, the Spirit begins to take form, begins to thrust, begins to evolve into complexities and perhaps into cohesiveness. This God seems to want consciousness in a creature, who perhaps can come back to the Garden and unite the opposites inherent in the nature of Yahweh, good and evil. Here is energy wanting to be related to creatures, moving toward the possibility of co-creation. Here is evolving, necessary because of the ambivalence and because the opposites themselves cannot be united without someone to unite them, and it is quite obvious that they cannot be united without the help of a creature. The Spirit is moving, toward or in relation to creatures in substance, in a transformative way. All of the Hebrew Scripture can be understood as a dialogue between God and creatures. It is a complex story, and in no sense can I do justice to it. Let me merely touch a few highlights that bear particularly on the purpose of creation and the purpose of the Spirit.

Why did Yahweh put a mark on the forehead of Cain so Cain would not be killed after he had murdered? Why did God want Cain saved? What was God's relationship to darkness at that point? Why was it important that Cain was saved?

Or look at the idea of the covenant first found in the story of Noah. It is a tremendously rich concept—that is the essence of Judaism in its deepest sense—that of the covenant between God and creature. After the flood, after Noah had built an altar and offered the burnt sacrifice, it says:

> And when the Lord smelled the pleasing odor, the Lord said in his heart, "I will never again curse the ground . . ." Behold, I establish my covenant with you and your descendants . . . and with every living creature . . . This is the sign of the covenant which I make . . . I set my bow in the cloud, and it shall be a sign of the covenant between me and the earth. When I bring clouds over the earth and the bow is seen in the clouds, I will remember my covenant . . ." "When the bow is in the clouds, I will look upon it and remember the everlasting covenant . . ." (Gen. 8:21-9:16)

It is as if Yahweh knows that He could forget the fundamental thrust of His own Spirit, as if He knows that the darkness is there and that He could forget, not just that creatures—persons, man, woman—could forget, but that He could forget, and so He makes the rainbow. I wonder if it is, perhaps, one of the first symbols of the Holy Spirit. It is there. And he makes a universal covenant with all living creatures.

We move from there to the book of Job, that wonderful book of the continual dialogue between Job and his God, and whose action Job struggled with, who certainly made possible the step that was to be taken later by Jesus. There is much one would like to quote from Job, but I have picked three places where Job is deeply concerned with the two sides of God. He is concerned with the fact that we must be responsible for both sides, both the good and the evil, the light and the dark. He says "all we receive good at the hand of God, and shall we not receive evil?" (Job 2:10). And he says, "Thy hands fashioned and made me; and now thou dost turn about and destroy me" (Job 10:8). And he says, "Behold, he will slay me; I have no hope; yet I will defend my ways to his face. This will be my salvation, that a godless man shall not come before him" (Job 13:15-16). To me that is one of the great statements anywhere in the Bible. So there is a tremendous sense of the struggle of Job with the Spirit of Yahweh, again in both of His aspects, His light and His dark side.

I turn now for a moment to Ezekiel the prophet. The Spirit of the Lord brings Ezekiel the prophet into the valley of dry bones, the valley of dead bones. And the Lord says to Ezekiel the prophet:

> Prophesy to these bones, and say to them, O, dry bones, hear the word of the Lord. Thus says the Lord God to these bones: Behold, I will cause breath to enter you, and you shall live. And I will lay sinews upon you, and will cause flesh to come upon you, and cover you with skin, and put breath in you, and you shall live; and you shall know that I am the Lord. (Ezek. 37:4-6)

First, sinews, flesh—further emphasis—and finally, breath. It is the story of the Spirit as an enlivening word, the Spirit coming into dead bones, the Spirit beginning to have a resuscitating influence and giving breath to the prophet as the Son of man who can act as part of this resuscitating process. What does this all say? It says a Spirit—active, yearning, restless, moving—wanting a creature to become conscious so that the Spirit may in fact be known, not being able to know Him/Herself without a human. And I am reminded again of the passage from the Jewish Midrash: "May it be my will that my love overcome my wrath." A wonderful statement, not only of the opposites—that wrath and love are there—but the hope that even God has, that His/her will is to be on the side of overcoming wrath, hostility, negativity, by love or through love. Perhaps it could be said that God is longing for reconciliation through the Holy Spirit.

Looking back over what we have discussed, we see that we have the two sides of Yahweh in the serpent and Yahweh; we have the bipolarity of the Tree, the knowledge of good and evil; and we have the Spirit as a healing Spirit beginning to come toward Substance to work with creatures and to begin to resuscitate, to bring resurrection to the dead bones. The covenant theme is there. Jeremiah (31:33) says of the covenant: "I will write it upon their hearts." I will write the covenant upon their hearts. Upon your hearts, upon our hearts, upon my heart. So, it is moving more and more toward Substance.

I have tried in these few words to convey something about the nature of this God in the Hebrew Scriptures, aspects that we have lost today. This God needs to be recaptured by all of us, because we have not kept the two sides together, and thus we have caused havoc in ourselves and in the world.

Let us now move to the moment of history when somehow both sides, the human and divine, were ready for
some new step that I will call a quantum leap. Moses' experience of the "I Am" was a form of a quantum leap. The
most significant new step, however, both from the standpoint of God and the human, is when Jesus appears on the
scene at the baptism of John the Baptist. Now a new relationship is ready to be born. What did John the Baptist
preach? Again, that there were two elements—light and
dark, good and bad. The bad would be burnt up, the good
would be saved. It was that simple, it was that split apart.
In John's message you would only be saved if you entered
the waters for baptism unto the remission of sin. I call
these the penitential waters, the waters of repentance.
Jesus came to this movement either for his own needs of
repentance, or because he felt drawn to this unorthodox
movement, or for other reasons. But whatever the reason,
he came. And what happened to Jesus? Let me remind you
of the simple words of the text, simple because they are so
profound:

> And when he came up out of the water, immediately he saw the
> heavens opened and the Spirit descending upon him like a dove;
> and a voice came from heaven, "Thou art my beloved Son; with
> thee I am well pleased." (Mark 1:10-11)

These are the words that attempt to describe the experience of this person Jesus. "The heavens opened": a
lightning bolt, the image of a break, a tear; God, life, torn
apart for some new revelation, for something new to happen. All the old to be torn: heavens opened. Perhaps a huge
cosmic birth pang.

"The Spirit descending upon him like a dove." A still,
small voice. The Spirit descends here into creature, into
the creature Jesus. God becomes now connected through
the Spirit with one person first, later with others. The fire
in John's message, which was to be the destructive fire
that would burn up the bad, becomes not a destructive
flame, but now like a dove, because Jesus as a vessel offered something different from the human side. The fire,
perhaps, became a sacred flame, baptized in water, of
which he could say later in his life, "I came to cast fire upon

the earth" (Luke 12:49). The fire of John goes into the water with Jesus and emerges as the symbol of the dove. There's a very beautiful symbolic statement from Justin Martyr, one of the early Church fathers, which reads:

> When Jesus went down to the waters, fire was kindled in the Jordan; and when he was raised from the water the Holy Spirit came upon him as a dove.

So, the fire was kindled when he went down; the fire went down with him, but what came up was something different.

The opposites now of good and evil, inherent in John's message through this descent of the Holy Spirit, now become two sides of one reality. A reconciling symbol in the form of the dove now appears in the creature—is born inside the creature—and brings together these two sides. Something happens now which unites the opposites into a singleness, yet keeps the differentiation. This reconciling factor, symbolized by the Holy Spirit, is incarnated in the person of Jesus. Perhaps the Spirit becomes holy when it becomes lodged in the Substance of a creature. The word "Spirit" appears ninety times in the Hebrew Scriptures. "Holy Spirit" appears three times, but on the whole, of course, it is a New Testament phrase. Psychologically, then, at this moment, it is as if an aspect of God was ready to become more indwelling in the human, to relate to the Self or become the *imago dei*, the image of God. This *is* the descent of the Holy Spirit, this movement from the transcendent, from the beyond, down into the psyche. We will follow the implications of this for us later, but we need to understand the deeper religious and theological implications here.

At the same time as this descent, Jesus also had the experience of being a beloved son. God was now born in the Self, expressed in both the Holy Spirit and in sonship. Jung has said that the Trinity is one of the greatest steps in the differentiation of God. But here we are dealing not with a dogma, but with the experience behind it. Jesus is experiencing the differentiation of God, descending as the Holy Spirit and as a son being born inside him. That later does become the dogma of the Trinity in Christian thought. Actually, we have a quaternity in the Baptism experience—because the water as feminine symbol is there, and Darkness. It is very moving to recognize that Jesus was also internalizing the messianic, and that he never said "yes" or "no" to it or identified with it. He never said "yes" or "no" when he was asked about being the Christ. He related to it, but how is another story.

Following the descent of the Holy Spirit and its new relation to Substance, what did that Spirit do? It immediately "drove" or "led" (depending on whether one looks at Mark or Matthew and Luke) Jesus into the wilderness. This shows the intent and concern of the Spirit for consciousness, namely, that Jesus had to go into the wilderness to face choices—Satan, the dark side— immediately. The Spirit drove Jesus to face extremely difficult choices and alternatives in his so-called temptations in the wilderness. It has been said, "The Holy Spirit helps man to see the two sides of God." And that is exactly what happened when the Holy Spirit drove Jesus into the wilderness, where he now had to face, at a very conscious level, the decisions which were in front of him. This is why I choose to call the wilderness experience the *ascent* of the Holy Spirit, because it drives Jesus into an excruciatingly difficult conscious choice. It is ascent when there is movement from the depths inside into consciousness. When the Holy Spirit moves down into a person, it requires a response from the person. It takes an ego. It takes a person like Jesus not to leave the depths, but to be sure that the depths are manifested, incarnated, brought into actualization at the conscious level (Jesus used the term Son of man to describe that which helps the Holy Spirit to come into the conscious area). Again, one could say that the Holy Spirit is the communication from the divine to the human depth, bringing together the two sides in the human person, who has to face the choices those two sides present and arrive at some new place. This whole incident of descent and ascent is, for me, the paradigm for the functioning of the Holy Spirit. The Holy Spirit descends from the transcendent, from the all-inclusive, all-purposive two-sided God, into the substance of the human being, Jesus: here the human can move to reconciliation, and with the help of the Son of man can move into choice, and fulfill the original intent of God.

The Holy Spirit, then, can now be continually present in the psyche, and with the help of the human can continually enter it. This incarnating of Spirit reconciles the bipolarity of God. I am using the two alternatives or two opposites. If A and B are two things inside, two opposites, then the reconciling symbol, or the reconciling answer, is when something is found which is not the same as either of those two answers, but something new that emerges from both of them. This was happening in the wilderness. Jesus helped the Holy Spirit become specific in its flow from the transcendent into conscious, human personality. The Spirit, originally a breath, becomes more a thrust; incarnated in substance, not just limited to one person, but available for all of us (as Jesus later made abundantly clear).

The term "Holy Spirit" appears very few times in the synoptic Gospels, only three times that I think are surely historical. But the Holy Spirit dominated the whole life of Jesus and went with him straight through to the very end, to the Crucifixion itself. Let us look at the two places where the word appears on the lips of Jesus most authentically.

In Mark 3, Jesus is accused by some of the Scribes of deriving his power from Beelzebub, the prince of the devils. Jesus calls this charge a blasphemy against the Holy Spirit, which "has never forgiveness" (Mark 3:29)—one of the strongest statements Jesus ever makes. This is a sin that has never forgiveness. To know what is good and to *call* it evil is to cut oneself off from the Tree of the Knowledge of Good and Evil. It is very different from doing evil. If one is cut off from the evaluation of the Tree one cannot turn, which is the act of forgiveness. This shows what Jesus felt was his own relationship to the Holy Spirit and affirms his solid relationship to it, and also it affirms the original bipolarity in Genesis. If you cannot distinguish or purposefully don't distinguish, and call good "evil"—for your own purpose—then you have done something fundamental to the core of personality. Jesus said, You can say anything you want to about me, you can say anything

you want to about the Son of man, but you cannot say anything you want to about the Holy Spirit because this power
inside him was the Source out of which he acted and which
was the discriminating thrust from the Tree of the
Knowledge of Good and Evil. To condemn that would be to
cut oneself off from the Source itself.

In another place Jesus says,

> And when they bring you before the synagogues and the rulers and
> the authorities, do not be anxious how or what you are to answer or
> what you are to say; for the Holy Spirit will teach you in that very
> hour what you ought to say. (Luke 12:11)

The Holy Spirit here is teacher, wisdom, counselor,
available at times of crisis and choice and conflict. Jerome
says that Jesus spoke of "his mother, the Holy Spirit."
This brings in a sense of the spirit rooted deeply in experience as matter ("mother"). The fact that the Holy
Spirit is available to others is apparent here, because Jesus
is speaking to his disciples: Don't be anxious, the Holy
Spirit will tell you what to say. The Holy Spirit can appear,
can come to us inwardly, but it needs human discrimination in order that it does not merely flood us with archetypal material.

I would like to move immediately to the Crucifixion
and ask this question: Was the Holy Spirit present at the
Crucifixion? My own answer is "yes," centrally so, because it was the time when Jesus finally confronted the
problem of darkness to which he had been totally committed from the beginning, in his Baptism. The Crucifixion
is the place of his final confrontation with darkness for the
total incarnation of *both* sides of God. This would not have
been possible if he himself had not lived the resurrected life
of the Holy Spirit within and had not been able to make
this final act, at which time "the veil of the Temple was
rent in twain" (Mark 15:38), which symbolically may be
related to the heavens rent asunder earlier in the Baptism.
Throughout his life Jesus certainly acted from the deep in-
wardness of whatever the messianic thrust was for him,
the saving element within. He acted on the will of God with
passion in situations and inwardly. Most central to me,
however, is how the Holy Spirit was really the crucial thing

that was newly there, which guided him because of its emergence with a new possibility of incarnation. I think this is exactly what happened when it came inside and became then the dove or the love, whereby all things could be integrated outside and inside.

What happened after the Crucifixion? Whatever happened to the disciples, certainly something—Jesus, Christ, Self, God—came alive in them. Then there was Paul, even before the Gospels, whose experience led to the doctrine of the risen Christ. Here the Christian myth begins, where Jesus now carries and is identified with the Christ. This meant that he also in a sense carried the Holy Spirit. If you read Paul and Acts and the Gospel of John you see that certainly there was a tremendous experience, but also a lack of clarity, archetypally, on the interpretation of the realities. Jung is surely right in pointing out that in the formation of the dogma of the Trinity, of the Father, the Son, and the Holy Spirit, there was a central differentiation in the God-image. In the dogma both Satan as adversary and the feminine were omitted from the Godhead, and this omission has characterized the whole Christian development. But there are two very important references in the early Christian literature to the Holy Spirit. In the second chapter of Acts there is the report of the day of Pentecost. In condensed form, it reads:

> When the day of Pentecost had come, they (the disciples) were all together in one place. And suddenly a sound came from heaven like the rush of a mighty wind, and it filled all the house where they were sitting. And there appeared to them tongues as of fire, . . . and they were all filled with the Holy Spirit and began to speak in other tongues, as the Spirit gave them utterance. (Acts 2:1-4)

What is the difference between this experience and the experience of Jesus at the Baptism? Here it is a group, whereas with Jesus it was an individual; here it is, in a sense, a collective happening. With Jesus there was an entrance into the penitential waters, there was a step on the part of the creature; here it is fire and wind—in the Baptism, it is the dove—to bring together opposites in both God and person; here there is the possibility of archetypal inflation, of being taken over by fire and wind, versus the person as a vessel, ready to contain it; and, perhaps most crucial of all, here there is no wilderness experience afterwards, versus the wilderness experience of Jesus—and that may be a very central difference. The disciples didn't go to the wilderness in the same way that Jesus went to the wilderness. They didn't go to where they had choice, for although much happened afterwards in the area of choice, none was of the caliber that Jesus confronted in the wilderness.

Then we have in the Gospel of John the whole concept of the Paraclete, the assurance by Jesus in the Gospel that his words and teachings would be carried on, would be given to them by the Comforter, by the Paraclete.

As Pentecost can be looked on as the baptism for the disciples, the Paraclete, perhaps, can be looked on as that which carries the spirit and teachings of Jesus, as promised to them by him in the Gospel. Both of these experiences, of the Pentecost or the Paraclete, dynamically contain and are objects of belief. They are deeply Christian experiences, as opposed to the experience of Jesus. They assume the centrality of Jesus and Jesus' relation to the Holy Spirit and the Son, rather than, as Jesus did, the centrality of God and His/Her Holy Spirit.

The last incident to look at is the Virgin Birth. It is last, because it is probably the last mythic element to be added to the story. In Luke, the angel says to Mary, "The Holy Spirit will come upon you, and the power of the Most High will overshadow you . . . " (Luke 1:35). Here, the Holy Spirit becomes the impregnating element, joining with the feminine for the birth of the new son. Or, put another way, here the opposites of the masculine and feminine come together and the new, the son, is born out of it. It is fascinating that Russian Orthodoxy has a tradition of Mary being impregnated through the ear by the Holy Spirit; I add that because of all kinds of interesting possibilities about the relation of the ear to breath, and to hearing. It is important to relate the incident of the Virgin Birth to the Baptism experience. In both, the Holy Spirit comes as impregnating factor. In the Virgin Birth, the Holy Spirit comes into the feminine, into Mary; in the Baptism, the Holy Spirit comes into water and through that into Jesus.

Out of both experiences, a son is born. One is the experience of a son lived by Jesus, giving us a paradigm for conscious relationship, and the other is the experience of a son as a deep, inner, archetypal reality.

For me, the soundest relationship to the Holy Spirit resides for us in the experience of Jesus. Jung has said that it is the opposites *within* God that have to be reconciled now, not God with persons. The Holy Spirit by itself, without being in substance, can lead to fragmentation, extreme irrationality, along certainly—with some healing. The Holy Spirit, if it is related to substance in ourselves, is really somehow in our own being, if we work over and over to touch it there. We will find that it will yield for us, through its constant descent and its constant ascent, a third point for our everyday decisions and our everyday work of integration. This assumes the commitment that I think Jesus is talking about as that of choices, alternatives, conflicts, different possibilities, in the search for what is really the deepest value in every situation. If we also see that inside our own psyches we are full of conflicting opposites, and we have to look at those opposites, we will also find a healing center. If we can work at these areas in our own individual evolutions, then it can be said we are working with the Holy Spirit. It is in this sense that I would say that the Holy Spirit is not a hasty or overwhelming shout or message, but a task to be chosen—ever new, ever fresh, ever mysterious, transformative for a Thou who wants it and transformative for a person who wants it.

Transformation in the Life of Jung

I was asked to speak on the background and development of the events that shaped the ideas of Dr. Jung. It
feels redundant to quote the outer facts of his life, which
are available in many books and films. The major concepts of libido, opposites, complementarities, the four func-
tions, introversion/extraversion, archetypes, symbols, the
collective and personal unconscious, the objective psyche,
and projection—these are increasingly a part of the
language of our society today. Sometimes they are used
properly, sometimes improperly.

But it will not be presumptuous to speak of the nodal
points in his thinking that influenced his own religious
growth. It helps to see the repercussions of these in the
fields of the healing professions and in theological explora-
tions. It is also significant to look at the resistance to Jung
from both the psychologists who consider him too religious, and the religionists who consider him too psychological. It is also necessary to reflect on some of the dangers at
this moment of history.

I have been an analyst in the Jungian tradition for
many years, have helped found and lead seminars under
the Guild for Psychological Studies, with special emphasis
on Jung's contribution to an understanding of the life and
teachings of Jesus, the Hebrew Scriptures, and mythic material. It was a privilege for me to have been able to talk
both alone and in small groups with Jung, and especially
to have personal analysis with Mrs. Jung, for whom I had
enormous respect and admiration. I also have a good
friendship with some of his children. My background with

* Presented as keynote speech at conference on "Jung, Rebirth, and
You," Lloyd Center of San Francisco Theological Seminary, San
Anselmo, California, May 13, 1974.

Jung is quantitatively limited, but richly productive. This man consistently impressed me. He was a person of great stature, but very human. He stood eye to eye with you; his eyes twinkled and were sad alternately; his mouth held strength and tenderness; and he had the ability to go straight to the core of the subject, in direct confrontation and intensity. He had the talent to honor both the individual and the mystery behind the individual.

I have picked out four nodal points to discuss. Central, of course, was his break from Freud, the man who presented the unconscious as an iceberg and who started the revolutionary rediscovery of the unconscious. Jung broke from him as a mentor, because Freud did not go as deep as Jung desired to go. Jung, through patient scientific and diagnostic work, went on to expand the concept of the unconscious sphere from being merely a layer of the psyche that was repressed by the ego, as in Freud's description, to also include the collective level. Jung saw the unconscious as the reservoir of the archetypes, an eternal preserver of patterns out of which mythologies, religious experiences, and artistic creation flowed.

This level of depth had been known by great religious and mystical figures (most especially Jesus), and by artists and poets throughout history; but today too many have become cut off from it. This is perhaps more true of Protestants than of Catholics.

Two early dreams of Jung, reported in his autobiography, *Memories, Dreams, Reflections*, certainly foreshadowed this earth-shaking discovery. I quote them in a condensed form:

> When I was three or four, I was in a meadow and a huge stone-lined hole opened up. Hesitantly I descended down the hole and found a doorway covered by a heavy curtain. I pushed it aside and saw a long rectangular chamber with a rich golden throne in the center on a red carpet. Standing on it was a huge thing, reaching almost to the ceiling, made of skin and naked flesh and on top was a rounded head with no face and no hair.

How this original image faced him, with many dark phallic things, symbolically cannot be explained here.

The other dream occurred when he was ten or eleven and struggling with religious problems concerning the

Church, his relation to his father, and the role of darkness in the God and Christ image.

> I saw before me the cathedral, the blue sky. God sits on His golden throne, high above the world and from under the throne an enormous turd falls upon the sparkling new roof, shatters it, and breaks the walls of the cathedral asunder.

Out of these the thread of destiny appeared, and he wrote that from this time on, the idea of God began to interest him.

This breakthrough and slow revealing of the depth of the unconscious led Jung to a startling revamping of Freud's concepts. That is, the incest complex and what is behind it.

The character of the second nodal point I would describe as a time of courage. Out of his beginning breakthrough came the challenge of personally facing the deep opposites of the internal world at a time when there was no one to help him, and impersonally to be willing to defend his point of view to a scientific world not ready yet to be so stretched. His courage at this point moves me as much as anything about him. Had he not had a genuine and ruthless self-knowledge of his own objective psyche he would have gone under, as he makes clear in *Memories, Dreams, Reflections*. This was the time when he could do very little in his outer world. And one must remember his years of attempts to dialogue with his father, who was a rigid pastor with an orthodox viewpoint. Because of Jung's willingness to follow his destiny and not to flinch, we have available to us, for the internal journey, tools that help bring the unconscious to consciousness and manifestation.

These inner realities, especially of the shadow and darkness, were encountered with courage and with a commitment of no small dimension. At Bollingen, his home away from Kusnacht and family pressures, he chiseled from stone many faces and figures that described for him his life and its meaning.

The third decisive nodal point was, I believe, his journey to the discovery or rediscovery of the Self as the central archetype of meaning, integrating all other archetypes. It had about it a quality of purposiveness and teleology. Jung began to define individuation as the expression of the unique quality of Self encountered by the ego. Thus the healing process becomes a journey of rediscovery of the lost parts of the psyche that want reunification. He also saw all neurosis as a religious problem, a lack of meaning resulting from the psyche being out of balance. From the Self come reconciling symbols of integration and reconciliation.

I call this "nodal," because it meant a revision of the concept of the healing process and the demand of the "healer" to participate deeply in this process very early. The symptoms usually regarded as pathological were seen by Jung as elements in the psyche that needed work of a transformative kind by both "healer" and "patient." This involved a total restructuring of wound and healing. The experience and discovery of the Self archetype led Jung to the exploration of the heresies of alchemy and Gnosticism, and to venture such a thing as his *Seven Sermons to the Dead.*

The fourth nodal point (still very much in the process of being understood) is the profound concept of the psychoid factor and synchronicity as the relation of spirit and matter, and the *unus mundus.* In *Memories, Dreams, Reflections* he wrote that in his effort to depict the limitations of the psyche he did not mean to imply that *only* the psyche exists. He therefore even hazarded the postulate that the phenomenon of archetypal configurations may be founded upon a *psychoid* base, that is, upon an only partially psychic and possibly altogether different form of being.

Let me now examine in more detail the religious implications of all these steps, why there has been such resistance to Jung, and why and how it is now slowly changing. Dr. Jung attempted in his exploration to remain a scientist and to investigate the phenomena available in the psyche, and not the transcendent realities behind it. But the words over his house at Kusnacht, *Vocatus atque non vocatus, deus aderit* (Evoked or not, God is present), and my own impression in talking with him of his desire to talk of God, gave evidence of his deep religious concern.

Jung's rediscovery of the unconscious depths was followed immediately by his perception of the significance of the symbol, understood as expression in the form of the deep, inner power. Symbol conveys mystery as sign does not. Because our religious symbols have become so empty and there is such a lack of understanding of what they represent in the psyche, our religious life has, to a large extent, become barren. It is hard to face this inadequacy of symbols, especially in regard to the feminine and the dark side. It is beyond the scope of this talk to see how Jesus himself related to these opposites in the messianic-Christ image.

Another implication of Jung's discoveries was to find the psychological-mythic realities behind the theological ideas and formulations as they are manifested in creed and liturgy. The substance out of which dogma comes could now be understood as the archetypal level, and thus enlivened as real experience. One would not have to "believe," but to "know" this inner world. This applied most especially to a possible new experience behind the word "Christ" or "Jesus Christ." (This included the need to understand projection.) The possible recovery of real experience of this reality might well be a rallying point of a thrust forward in the theological field. But, in fact, this possible recovery has caused some of the deepest resistance because it challenges change from an intellectual or spiritual ideal about the person of Jesus to the search in oneself for the potential psychic reality to be related to and lived.

A further implication is seeing or understanding the Self as the image of God within, not to be identified with God. This separation of God and God in Self is even sometimes overlooked by Jungians themselves. The conflict between Jung and Buber centered on this; Buber accused Jung of identifying God and the Self and therefore being a Gnostic. But, as I pointed out earlier, Jung always confined his writing to the God-image. This God-image was for Jung whole and contained all the opposites, as Christianity has not done. This is vital to know in order to understand some of the resistances to Jung. In my last personal conversation with Jung at Ascona, we were talking of prayer, and he made a remark to me which has felt central and belonging to persons beyond me. He said, "And don't forget when you pray, to bring your darkness to God because that is what He needs." This was shocking, but became clearer and clearer as I realized he was talking of the kind of incarnation needed by God today—one of the totality and not the one-sided image.

Finally, I would mention Jung's emphasis on perseverance in the journey. Some of us start the journey and then transfer journeys to our patients or pastors or mentors and watch them, and live through them. Mrs. Jung once said to me, "It is psychic suicide to start the journey and then stop." To continue on will involve facing suffering in personal and professional situations. But it is just this ability to face suffering that leads to the growth of Love. It means facing our substance and integrating the contents into the whole.

What are the dangers today in regard to Jung's psychology? That he is coming to be known and accepted is obviously true. Sometimes I think of my first visit to Zurich in 1948, the year the Institute started. Jung did not want the Institute, yet it seemed necessary for the development of his work. It presented questions and dangers. What are these? An outstanding one for many individuals is that of inflation, because of the very nature of the unconscious and its dynamic symbols. It is all too easy to get lost in the Spirit or the Self as archetype, and to forget the role of the ego or to forget the God that is transcendent behind the Self, and the God operative in human situations. The Spirit can take us away from our true Substance.

At the impersonal level is the danger that Jungian ideas can become rigidified and codified, taking the place of experience of the unconscious. Seeing and knowing about the unconscious is not the same as experiencing it. "I know my shadow" does not necessarily include working at its transformation. There can be a tendency to forget Mrs. Jaffe's statement that "Jung's psychology is a psychology of consciousness, not of the unconscious." It is easier to be lost in a project outside rather than to encounter it inwardly. Even in dream work, it is not enough to know the symbols if the ego is not working at their assimilation.

I want to end with a few personal observations about the vision for the future. These come from my impressions in talks with Jung, and they seem to be the cornerstone for the future. I was amazed once by his use of the word "will-power" as necessary for the ego to have for the discipline of the journey. It is an old-fashioned word that we need.

The distinction Jung made late in his life between the wholeness and specificity of personality seems essential to true understanding. The specificity of one's Self was an achievement and expressed the unique, once-only creativity in each person.

The challenge to us all resides in the title of this conference—"Jung, Rebirth, and You." He made discoveries, but the integration is for each of us. In a letter, Jung wrote that God needs man to become conscious, just as he needs limitations in time and space, an earthly tabernacle. Dr. Jung was a good earthly tabernacle. More important is the question, Are *we*, each one of us, a strong tabernacle? Only so is the ongoing process of God served, manifested in our lives and society.

New Symbolic Meanings in Liturgy, Creed, and Prayer

In a recent talk to the Community of the Holy Spirit, an Anglican priest said: "Everything is going through a period of renewal except the Church." In a letter, the late Bishop Kilmer Myers wrote: "I am fearful of one possible development—the loss of the sense of the mysterium in our worship. One cannot plan a service of worship in order that the mystery will be revealed. Rather one must open oneself to the mystery, and this requires discipline."

For two thousand years the liturgical forms, creeds, and prayers of the Church have expressed the numinous depth of religious reality. These central sacred forms, whether articulate or not (especially in the Eucharist), have represented deep psychic tendencies of the human soul to participate in a religious reality greater and more purposive than its conscious, limited human world, a reality that reaches above and below, inside and outside.

Because this has been for so long intrinsically true about the sacred forms, people have been able to participate in them, to be moved and inspired by them, and somehow to be altered by them for a shorter or a longer period of time. These structures, especially in the Catholic church, have been true containers for the archetypal depths in the human, whether conscious or not. If people are unknowingly not connected with their inner depths, then the liturgical forms and symbols eventually will not speak to them.

Dr. Esther Harding in the 1959 issue of *Spring* wrote: "The symbols of Christianity have lost their power to influence mankind because they have been undermined by the rationalistic spirit and scientific materialism of the last

* *Presented at Grace Cathedral in San Francisco, California, in 1971.*

one hundred and fifty years of Western thought. As a result, people no longer need to participate in the mysteries of their religion." If the liturgical form and its symbols do not represent the psychic depth, then nothing is moved in those participating. The crisis of the Church seems to me to center first in the loss of the ability to arouse this *Tremendum* in people and also in the failure to help people understand the implications even when it is aroused. Either the old symbols must be revitalized through self knowledge and the arts, or new liturgical symbols must be discovered so people can become more conscious rather than more rational.

To facilitate the exploration of the means and possibilities in this area, I would like to say a few fundamental words about Dr. Carl Jung's discoveries. I would also like to describe some contributions possibly beyond or different from Jung, concerning the Gospels and religious practices. The single greatest discovery of Jung, when he parted with Freud, was his demonstration of the existence of a religious depth in personality, of a level of universal or archetypal images, the collective unconscious versus the purely personal level of Freudian repressed subconscious content. Jungian archetypes are primordial images that do not consist of inherited ideas, but of predispositions to reactions in universal situations. They are "eternal presences" in the soul, and they express themselves by projection into symbols. Thus the symbol, if alive, always presupposes an unknown and deeper mystery which cannot be explained rationally. The great archetypes include the mother; the father; the savior; the divine child; the devil; the journey of transformation; death and rebirth; and the Self as the center of personality, the integrative process including all our opposites, which Jung calls the God image.

In *Psychology and Religion* Jung wrote that religious experiences are facts which demonstrate the existence of an authentic religious function in the unconscious. The fact is that certain ideas exist almost everywhere. They are not made by the individual. They just happen to him — they even force themselves on his consciousness. The term "religious" designates the attitude peculiar to a consciousness which has been changed by the experience of the *numinosum*. Creeds are codified and dogmatized forms of the original religious experience.

Individuation is defined by Jung as the commitment of the ego (the center of the conscious personality) to relate to all the parts of the unconscious as a requisite to finding the real Self, the uniqueness of each person which nonetheless rests on a shared Center. Hans Schaer, the eminent European theologian, has written in *Religion and the Cure of Souls in Jung's Psychology*, that rediscovery of the Self is nothing less than a new revelation of God—not the only one, but an inner one which the Church has too long ignored. This central Self, as the "other" within, also contains manifold opposites, a fact to be noted as a contrast to the Christian split that has sundered the Self. We believe in God and brotherhood, yet we napalm thousands of helpless people and pollute the whole globe. We could give many equally brutal personal examples of this denial of wholeness within.

The inner aspects of the psyche most neglected today are the feminine principle and the problem of evil. When we left the early mother religions for the development of Judaism, and when we left Catholicism for the Reformation, we left behind us the major embodiments of feminine wisdom. Luther attempted to keep alive the symbolic meaning of the Virgin as feminine principle, and certain attitudes within the Anglican tradition reflect a similar emphasis. The teachings of Jesus are filled with insights into the positive feminine principle. (Not the woman but the feminine!)

The question of darkness and the Self, or darkness in the Self, is a pivotal question in the light of the vast amount of evil in the world. Where does darkness come from? Humans or God? Is the Christ/Anti-Christ split of Revelation the same as what Jesus had to say about evil? Did he split evil from the God reality? One main question Jung has raised is that the dogmatic Christ of Christian history as carrier of the Self has not been broad and inclusive enough of all the opposing tendencies of the psyche. He would feel that generally it had been too identified with the light, bright side.

Jung traces religious forms and concepts to these psychic roots inside human beings, but this in no way detracts from the mystery behind them. He says that the archetype does not circumvent the Christian mystery. Jung is sometimes accused of denying the transcendent. He sometimes used the term to speak of the deep, objective level *in the psyche from which healing and reconciling symbols come.* But he never denied the reality behind the archetype. He never confused the God image with God.

What is the relation of these psychological considerations to ritual and liturgy? The function of ritual can be seen as the attempt to give form to these inner realities. What is within our control is what we will do with this interior world. If we do not choose to help integrate and channel it, it becomes very negative and dissociates us and the outer world into pieces. There is no meaningful ritual left.

Jung writes that there is a dissociation extending throughout the entire world, a psychological split in vast numbers of individuals and in the iron curtain outside which reflects the inner split. We see it in the black-white problem of projection of the shadow. We see it in the current "Jesus " and "Satan" cults. We see the positive and negative side of the revolt in young people—the positive of the unconscious coming up in artistic, creative expressions, the negative in the whole drug scene.

The problem is that of putting a new ethic of inclusion or inclusiveness in place of the old ethic of dualism, of the perfectionist split between opposites. The Church has tended to be on the side of the old ethic—and Jesus was on the side of the new ethic. The Church today needs to be on the side of inclusiveness rather than of repression and perfectionism. In the light of these observations, let me return to the Church and its effectiveness in leading people to the depth where the gripping mystery is at work, or could be. The Episcopal, on the borderline between Catholic and Protestant, has a unique opportunity of maintaining symbol and ritual as living realities.

A consideration of three areas central to our religious life, which show the deeper personal and psychic meanings behind the Cross and Crucifixion, the Eucharist, and prayer, may help concretize the foregoing. I have chosen these out of a wealth of possibilities such as the Virgin Birth, the Trinity, the Baptism, and so on.

It must be emphasized again that looking at psychological meanings of religious processes is just the opposite of belittling them. It honors them as individual realities. Jung says that to treat a metaphysical statement as a psychic process is not to say it is merely psychic, as my critics would assert in the fond belief that the word psychic postulates something known. It does not seem to have occurred to people that when we say the psyche, we are alluding to the most dense darkness it is possible to imagine. The ethics of the researcher requires him to admit when his knowledge comes to an end. This is the beginning of true wisdom.

The cross itself is, of course, a central mandala, a symbol, an archetype signifying wholeness that belongs in the category of all great fourfold symbols found in Christian, Navajo, Tibetan, Chinese, and other religions. Think for a minute of the basic things in the universe that are divided into four—the four seasons, the four points of the compass, the four evangelists, the four rivers in Eden, and so forth. The very structure of many church buildings has traditionally been in the form of a cross, for example, the transept and nave in Western Christianity.

And in modern forms the four still remains, even if not as a cross, as in the new Saint Mary's Cathedral in San Francisco. The whole history of church architecture and its development relative to the various cruciforms is significant and fascinating. The symbolism of four in the cross is highly charged, containing as it does the tension of opposites—the vertical and horizontal dimensions, the God-human and interhuman relation. It has form and order as opposed to the continual flux of the psyche. For Christianity in general, I would say the dimension of the cross most ignored is the downward vertical thrust—the divine going into the earth as opposite to the divine going into the heavens—going into matter itself, into the deep sources.

When we move from the cross to the man on the Cross, we have a dynamically enlarged configuration. Now, regardless of what term we use, we have a Man, Son of Man, God in Man, God become Man, bearing the suffering of the opposites and being crucified for them. Something is now happening to both Man and God.

Early in his ministry Jesus said, "If any man would come after me, let him deny himself, and take up his cross, and follow me" (Matt. 16:24, Mark. 8:34, Luke 9:23). He did not say: "Follow my cross." He did not say: "Follow me." He said specifically to take up our own and follow. We have very little understanding of what it means to take up our own cross, the burden and gift of our individuation. We have preferred *imitatio Christi*, to try to be like him instead of risking becoming ourselves, or to be the way God wants us to be, which Jesus himself actually preached.

To take up our own cross presupposes a great deal of Self-knowledge, which we dread. As Jung says, Self-knowledge means that the Self factor in us must become conscious. This is seen specifically in the analytic process. The confrontation with ourselves as a religious process demands great courage, and we can avoid it as long as things are projected outside. We need individually to be involved in the process of Self-searching to know objectively the need for wholeness and all inclusiveness, not perfection. We need to know where we lack or are one-sided in such pairs of opposites as masculine/feminine, active/passive, strong/weak, confident/insecure. Above all we need to face in specific terms in our own lives the most extreme pair of opposites, symbolized in the cross—that of good and evil, light and dark. It is easy to acknowledge sin in the abstract. It is very difficult to face it in the concrete. For the devil, or the demonic, is least integrated or understood by us, which is why we project so much evil outside today. But did not Jesus continually face darkness all his life, finally choosing to be killed by it in order to help in its transformation?

What was Jesus' own relation to darkness as different from the dogmatic Christ's relation, theologically? We can only revitalize the symbol of the cross and the Man on the Cross as a symbol of ultimate commitment to transformation by our own searching. I find in both clergy and laity today a great dearth of involvement with the Cross in any way that really touches any human depth and the question of what the Incarnation can mean in a life. We simply are not seized and gripped by it in its numinosity and specificity. The central religious figure of our faith needs revitalization. Recently I spoke to a clergyman who despaired, "I need a Jesus who really is earthy and gutty and has some meaning, and not this pure, sinless figure, all so antiseptic!"

Turning to the Eucharist, I can only suggest a few things in the presence of this central mystery. Dr. Jung wrote that the Mass is the whole individuation process in the unconscious because it transforms the soul of the empirical man who is only a part of himself into his totality symbolically expressed in Christ. Its whole sequence represents the soul's development, but is unconscious. The sequence of events in the Mass contains a representation, in condensed form, of the life and sufferings of Christ.

Perhaps no feature of the Church is undergoing more outer change, in the interest of helping it become more meaningful to people, than the Eucharist. One cannot help but wonder, however, whether some of the forms today come perilously close to taking away the mystery and bringing it too much to a human level only. This feels very negative. Yet it is not easy to articulate specific changes that can help make it more redemptive.

Where might our own self-reflection about the elements begin to help actualize in ourselves the meaning of these tremendous symbols? Why have the grain and grape made into bread and wine been such great symbols in pagan, Greek, Jewish, and Christian religions? We know this but we forget. No two things could more represent the work of devotion to transformation, for both are products of earth worked on by humans with patience and perseverance. They have undergone transformation through leavening or fermentation. They are the symbols par excellence of God-given substance transformed into joyful products by sun, darkness, rain, and the human. They are symbols of the change from natural to supranatural. Each time we partake, do we meditate on this concretely?

In the terms of alchemy, the wisdom of the ancient physicians of the soul, what of our own substance, our *prima materia*, is being transformed into the stone, the lapis, the gold? All this part of the meditation is prior to the Christian aspect of the mystery.

Second, we have the bread and wine becoming the "body and blood." As I understand the use of the word, the Eucharist may be understood as for the "Anemnesis of Me," the "re-calling and re-energizing in the Christ of the one Sacrifice," according to Gregory Dix, in *The Shape of the Liturgy*—not many sacrifices, but one.

This seems to be a very archetypal statement of re-arousing the original meaning of the Event. In *Psychology and Religion Vol. II*, Dr. Jung has written that the Mass endeavors to include the believer in the process of transformation. It tries to effect a *participation mystique*—or identity—of priest and congregation with Christ so that on the one hand the soul is assimilated to Christ, and on the other hand the Christ-figure is recollected in the soul. It is a transformation of God and man alike, since the Mass is, at least by implication, a repetition of the whole drama of Incarnation.

One fundamental question can be raised as to why people today do not find the Eucharist more gripping. One reason is that the central Christ figure whose sacrifice is recalled has lost the power he once had, and so the "body and blood" of that figure does not move people as it once did. The whole Eucharist depends on the "Anemnesis of Me"—but who is the Me, the Christ?

Perhaps we need to understand and feel a rearousal of what is behind the "body and blood sacrifice." We must remember that there are two accounts of Jesus at the Passover meal. In Luke 22:15-18, according to some manuscripts, Jesus does not partake of the bread and wine, and gives no reference to these as symbols of his body and blood.

And what exactly was the relation of human, Jesus, the Christ image, and God? Perhaps a shift is possible— perhaps an understanding of Jesus here and at Gethsemane and on the Cross could become, in a fresh way, the paradigm of total commitment, choice, and risk.

Somewhere this may have some depth of symbolic meaning, in spite of the fact that, of course, the wine and bread as body and blood have had deep archetypal meaning through the centuries. It has been a moving experience to me to see these symbols and their mystery become again—and in new ways—very alive for people who have studied in the seminars with me on the Life of Jesus. I say this only to show that when the figure is again alive, consciously or unconsciously, the symbol becomes alive. I suspect that to many church people the Christ figure isn't alive. A dream is an excellent example of the change to newness. A man who had been a church person earlier but not for years told me of this dream: "I returned to the church of my childhood, stood in the middle of the church, and the minister then baptized me all over with wine. I am deeply moved and know in the dream that it involves transformation for me."

Another fundamental question concerning the Eucharist is whether, in addition to not really knowing what the "body and blood" mean, we really know in a specific and challenging way the meaning and content of what we need to sacrifice. In the light of what we know today about the psyche, the phrase, "we offer these gifts to You, a perfect holy and living sacrifice," can be vague and even misleading. Genuine sacrifice means self-knowledge of what more exactly needs to be sacrificed and what needs *not* to be sacrificed for genuine individuality. A great deal of discrimination is needed here: When is anger to be renounced? When is it creative for wholeness? When are sexual problems to be faced, when sacrificed? When is repentance of certain acts a genuine mark of humility? When is it a rejecting act of repression? When do certain habits need transformation rather than to go on consuming our energy?

In *Psychology and Religion* Dr. Jung has written that to make a sacrifice is an act of self-recollection, a gathering of what is scattered—all the things in us that have never been properly related, and a coming to terms with oneself with a view of achieving full consciousness. (Unconscious self-sacrifice is merely an accident, not a moral act.) Self-recollection, however, is about the hardest and most repellent thing there is for man, who is predominantly unconscious. Human nature has an invincible dread of becoming more conscious of itself. Nobody can give what he has not got. So anyone who can sacrifice himself and forego his claim must have had it, i.e., he must have knowledge of the claim. The sacrifice proves that you possess yourself, for it does not mean just letting yourself be passively taken. It is a conscious and a deliberate self-surrender, which proves you have control of yourself, and your ego.

This is indeed the challenge to us. Turning to prayer, how can we put dynamic and refreshing meaning into it? (If time permitted, I would separate it from meditation and creative introversion, both of which are also vital to living.) Is one of the problems that people simply do not know what they are worshiping or to whom they are praying, because their concept of God needs so much revision? God is *not* dead, but is certainly in need of new definitions and dimensions, within and without. Is it also possible that much of traditional prayer, whether verbal, silent, contemplative, or whatever, has been repressive to the psyche? The spiritual aspect can be reached, indeed, even evoked; but this act may not necessarily reach the rest of the psyche, *unless* there is a committed ego that helps to relate all the parts to the Whole.

This is another significant discovery of Jung's: *the spiritual aspect* of the personality has the great danger of splitting off and therefore not leading to wholeness. The substance, the earthiness, the world of time and space: that opposite to Spirit needs to be included within prayer. This offers a whole and exciting new field of development of techniques with which the Guild is doing much experimentation. When people take seriously the statement of Jesus about dealing with anger only after you have been to the altar, they begin to bring together instead of splitting apart the realities of how they feel (not what they should feel) and work at the transformation of that into love, which the altar offers.

Prayer needs to be redefined as bringing all one's parts to the deepest healing Source, transcendent and immanent, without judgment, for *renewal and change*. This may sound like what we have always said and attempted, but in fact this is not the case. Far too many of the clergy have dealt with prayer by keeping many of their problems compartmentalized and isolated from prayer and their religious life, until finally forced to face them. It is good to remember that Jesus urges us to become aware of our anger at the altar, to go work at reconciliation with our brother or sister and return to the altar (Luke 22:42).

If we had a new understanding of what it meant to say "not my will but thine" (Luke 22:42), as a need to find and work toward the center within in order to bring more of the "all" to the everyday existential choices where the transcendent expresses itself in the situational, there might be a deeper response. If the clergy could lead in this direction, the laity might follow. Most of the time our prayers leave our fears, anxieties, egocentricities, and compulsions right where they were! It isn't because we haven't been sincere, but because we haven't understood whether, when we feel "Christ's presence," we are feeling something toward wholeness or toward perfection. How much have we been aware of what the Apostles Creed says if taken personally, inwardly, symbolically? How much do we take each sentence of the Lord's prayer and know its meaning? How much do we understand the great Requiem masses as archetypes of death and rebirth for us?

In conclusion, what seems most needed is to expand in psychological knowledge and experience of what religious living requires concerning the total psyche; to know we must plumb our own depths before helping others; to be willing to be open to change our concepts to include the inner (as is certainly happening in many things the Church is doing today on various fronts that wouldn't have been heard of fifteen years ago, such as the exciting new masses, and music); to be willing to take up our Cross as a conscious dismemberment and self-scrutiny out of which a new resurrection can come; to acknowledge how difficult Self-recollection and Self-knowledge is; and to understand how genuine consciousness increases the mystery, because it relates us to the irrational depths.

How can we begin to go about this? Deep work at our own unconscious in a religious way might be relevant not only for such clergy as would be interested, but would also richly further the growth of meaning in the Church. (This is quite separate from the whole question of the values and dangers of inadequately trained clergy as counselors today.) If clergy could experience their own unconscious, people in the church would know the renewal and grace of God as expressed in this woman's dream:

> I was walking on a path in a garden and suddenly saw coming toward me a grotesque and evil looking dwarfed man. I knew he intended me harm but there was no place to run. So I moved toward him and he grabbed me, to pull me down and harm me. I began to say the Lord's prayer and put my arms around him. He started to cry as did I, and we stood there reconciled. His evil had turned into relationship and grief and love.

Such people, plus others with their unique sense of God, could form the nucleus of work with religious forms and structures to enliven the thrust of Presence, of infusing new meaning into old forms of worship services, of using old music in new ways and new music in old ways. This cannot be put into the Church deliberately or rationally unless there are conscious people who know on their pulses something of the phenomena of symbol formation and projection and their religious values. In short, the contribution of Dr. Jung needs to be far more widely spread in theological and church circles.

The insights of religious depth psychology are needed if we are to recapture the lost essence of the message of Jesus. Paul Tillich said not long before his death that if Christianity is to be relevant, it must get back to the original Event, which was Jesus. And this Jesus, as he is studied in the approach of the Guild, is not the human Jesus opposed to or separated from the divine or Christ aspect, as is often meant although he is called Jesus. One possibly can get at the person Jesus in his own relatedness to the divine and the messianic, which may be different from the Christian picture.

There may be other far-reaching changes going on archetypally, of which Pope Paul's new dogma on the Assumption of Mary was a fine example. But also it may be that the Aquarian Age will require a new and possibly revolutionary picture of Jesus himself going through his own individuation process rather than primarily being only the object of Christian faith.

There may be a religion *of* Jesus in addition to a religion *about* Jesus. Seminar groups in this area have potential power for the activation of new symbols.

Today is the crisis not only of the Church, but of the planet. We, the planet Earth, will or will not survive depending on what we do with what we know, depending on whether we work consciously or let things remain unconscious and split and deteriorate, or transform them into healing and love. Whether the Church will perish or not may not be as important as whether the planet perishes. But if the latter happens, certainly the eye of God will hold a perplexed wonder as it looks on the Church, which supposedly had been the vehicle for the value that is God coming to birth in the human soul.

To risk *not* helping this process is to bring on the wrath of God (in the words of Jacob Boehme), instead of the love of God. God needs us co-creators, and for this we must know both where His/Her need for us is greatest today, perhaps incarnating Him/Her in our soul; and how the Mystery of His/Her grace and healing in and about us may be helped to permeate the crevices of our psychic being for our fulfillment, for the saving of the world, and for His/Her fulfillment and glory.

Religious Imagery and Jung

In a theological seminary lecture it seems appropriate to start with a consideration of what is behind the religious images that want to be heard, rather than by what or how we work with religious symbols and images. From where comes the cry inside us that expresses itself and wants to communicate to our conscious side? What is the mystery of the world of the Other inside us? What aspect of the immanent divine speaks with intensity and urgency in us? What aspect of God neglected by the Church needed a Freud and a Jung to bring to our attention the depths of the psyche where the divine also dwells, in addition to psychic depths in history? Prophets, mystics, and great religious artists have surely known the answer, but somehow they have become forgotten in that place where they should most be carried, namely in the churches. What does the inner world want of each of us? And what do I want or need of that inner world? The transcendent God who furthers wholeness and healing speaks in more than one way. Jung was concerned with the way that God spoke through the psyche. Thus I stress that in our inner selves we are dealing with one of the aspects of the divine, and the need of God, which perhaps we and the Church need to listen to.

This inner world of gods and goddesses and God, this invisible world of reality, is always touching us, influencing us, impinging upon us, wanting our response to help it become actualized and manifested in ourselves and in history. As Jung tells us over and over, this world of depth of inner being wants incarnation in us. It wants to become

* Presented at the San Francisco Theological Seminary, San Anselmo, California, 1975.

and it speaks primarily through religious images and images in the world of art. It wants to step over—that
dynamism inherent in the God thrust within invisible life,
and it needs our aid to do so. I struggle to say this as clearly
as I can. I see a stained glass window in a cathedral. I hear
a Bach mass. I read a poem by Rilke. I see a rose garden. I
dream a dream. How do I respond? What did the creator of
the window, the mass, the poem, the producer of the roses,
or the dreams, intend to express? What does it say to me?

I can go behind these questions and stand in the presence of any one of these creations. For instance, I might
take the rose window of Chartres and say, "This is a moving symbol to me," meaning that it carries some mystery
of my own psyche that I see in it. But I can also go on to
say, "What does it mean that this is within me, this reality
that makes this a symbol? Why does it desire to become
visible?" Here the depths of the divine urge add a dimension to my own desire to respond. Let's think for a minute
of the beginning of the Genesis myth: God created man in
his own image; in his own image created he them." If this
be true, then logically our inner world must include the
whole spectrum of God, the totality of the Other. Jung says
in several of his letters that the Creator sees himself
through the eyes of man's consciousness. And Meister Eckhart, one of the great mystics and one of Jung's favorite
mystics, says God is not blessed in His Godhead. He must
be born in persons forever. This puts our creation, our
birth, each of us, in a very different perspective. Our work
with religious images must be the way we help that which
is behind the images that come to birth, that which wants
to cross over from the invisible into the visible life. All of
the evidence in Jung's letters and in *Memories, Dreams,
Reflections*, points to his discovery and evaluation of this
inner world as a religious world. And out of it he came to
the conclusion that the discovery of the unconscious is a
spiritual task. We know from his books of his struggle and
break from Freud. His great courage was to meet objectively what was there in the depths, and to make major
changes of Freud's system. He put the unconscious prior,
and saw the libido and the nature of the unconscious as in-
finitely more than the sexual libido, and included religious

and spiritual aspects. From his own experience, and then from his research into other people's dreams, into myths, into fairy tales, into the mysteries of Gnosticism and alchemy, the field of art—all this research led him to be able to assert the universality of deep eternal presences, or what he called archetypes—universal presences dressed in different clothes at different times of history and in different cultures. These universal presences expressed through the language of symbol are carriers, or focal points of energy, in the unconscious. He discovered from all these fields of research that he could assert the presence of these archetypes in their different garbs in the psyches of all humans. The dark unknown is the womb of forms, the womb from which artistic and religious forms are born. Many creative forces are in the darkness, instinctual forces we have repressed, as well as regressive forces and possibly evil itself. But much of the unknown can become creative.

The archetypal contents that Jung discovered included the masculine and feminine. "Created he them" not only man and woman, but also masculine and feminine in all of us. Also included is the idea of the psychological journey. Thus there is a way—whether you call it a way for salvation, redemption, or integration—a universal presence inherent in our very structure. There is also the wounded healer or savior as the saving element within. There is, for Jung, the Self which he speaks of as the *imago dei*, the inner image of God. He never called the Self "God" but sees the image of God as the integrative central archetype, which contains the possibility of reconciliation of all the opposites in the psyche. Space does not allow all of the archetypes to be named, but some of the main ones are masculine/feminine, darkness, the journey, the wounded healer, the Self. I hope that I have made clear at least the relation of the psyche to the religious process as a whole and something of the contents of the psyche.

We need now to look at the wide range of religious symbols. Because of this central concern, Jung struggled with the adequacy or inadequacy of Christian symbolism as it has come fundamentally through the ages, and where it is today. I trust that we understand the mechanism whereby our unknown hidden psyche (that which wants to become visible) is projected into things, into objects, into people, who then become the symbols for those contents. As we come to know ourselves and the things that relate to ourselves inwardly, we come to relate to our own depths. The symbols carry the mystery of the unknown.

You are probably familiar with the well-known distinction Jung makes between the symbol and the sign. We know the meaning of the sign, and we know some of the meaning of a symbol, but we will never know all of the unfathomable depths that the symbol carries. Anything can become a symbol. We can project our inner images into almost anything. Certain modes, of course, are more apt to arouse the symbolic life and call forth response from us. What might some of these be? Some of them would be music, painting, poetry, all forms of art; words (especially important for religion or the Church), the power of the word; the area of nature itself—sun, moon, rock, water, flowers, mountain; and the strong emotions of love, and perhaps of hate, too. You might stop briefly and ask yourself, What is my own most important religious symbol? I'm not asking you to answer, I'm just asking you to think about it. What symbol most carries, whether in or out of the Church, the religious meaning for you? Ponder that for a minute. It is the function of a culture to learn the meanings of its symbols and to see whether they are adequate to express the depth of the psyche as it is known at any period of history.

I would now like to turn to Christian culture and the Christian era, to see why Christianity does not seem to express adequately the contents of the depths as Jung has helped us to rediscover them. Some of you certainly may feel that Christianity is totally adequate. However, if our symbols are not adequate to express our depths, then obviously we are neglecting that which we supposedly serve, the Other that is more than my narrow life or my ego; God in all God's aspects is somehow narrowed. If our symbols are not adequate for the depth that is in us, then not only are we as individuals limited, but that which is trying to express itself—whatever name you give to the Cry, the Other, the God—is limited. This is the crisis we are dealing with.

Perhaps the best way to evaluate the adequacy or inadequacy of a religious symbol is to look at the archetypal contents as Jung has helped us see them, and learn the way that these main archetypes have been symbolized, rejected, or distorted during these two thousand years. Have these archetypes in fact been carried adequately in our tradition? Jung makes the point that, because the symbols have not been adequate, we turn to the East instead of examining our own culture. Jung had no objection to learning from the East, but he was very concerned for our Western culture. He said that he was an avowed opponent of taking over yoga methods or Eastern ideas uncritically. He believed very deeply that we must root ourselves in our own Western tradition, even though it must be vastly expanded. Let us go back then to the list of the archetypes.

Masculine/feminine—perhaps it is easiest to begin there because it is uppermost today in the creative protest of the feminist movement. It is so much in the forefront that we hardly need dwell on it. I would add, however, that it is not just the women who have been neglected, but it is the whole feminine element in man and woman. I feel very deeply about this. For the Catholic on the whole, the figure of Mary has significance different than for Protestants. But even Mary—does she include, for instance, the value of Demeter, the value of Isis, the value of Sophia, all the pagan elements that have been carried by the goddesses? The feminine is everywhere but its totality has not been known. The new child must come from the feminine and the masculine. This is so self-evident we hardly need say it, and yet it is exactly that which we have never carried over into the spiritual or psychic life. The new child, new insight, new life must come from a union of the opposites of feminine and masculine, and not from just the one-sided masculine (as expressed, for instance, in the masculine Trinity).

We come then to the problem of darkness, most central today because of the personal and social implication of our neglect of it. As Jung has said over and over again, God and our Christ have on the whole become much too one-sided on the light side. Because we have so repressed our dark side it now explodes, and all the ways in which it explodes I hardly need point out to you. You only need to read the newspaper every morning in case you do not know it in your own psyche. But I hope you also know it a little bit in yourself. And I hope we do not know it only in ourselves, but also recognize the tremendous social implication of what we have done with the darkness. Because we do not take seriously our own wounds, our own hurts—even in children—they fester and they become our sins. Unattended to, our wounds turn into negative forces, hostility, and violence. The frightening statistics on brutality, not only to children but to adults, testifies to this. The explosion of darkness on a cosmic scale, particularly World War II, was what led Jung to be immensely involved with the question of the genesis and origin of evil.

Was evil only in the human, or was evil in the Self: and is evil also in God? This was the problem, as many of you know, that occupied Jung most in his later years. In my talks with him I certainly felt that. He struggled with the book of Job, where Job says: "Shall we receive good at the hand of God, and shall we not receive evil?" (Job 2:10). A far cry from where most of us are! Psalm 139:8 states, "If I ascend to heaven, thou art there! If I make my bed in Sheol, thou art there!" Jung's extensive discussion in his letters with Victor White, who was the leading Dominican Catholic priest influenced by Jung, showed their complete disagreement, inasmuch as White maintained only good was in God.

I recently led a weekend seminar on Paul Tillich, and I was again tremendously impressed. I keep wondering what theologians do with Tillich. In his book *The Courage to Be*, Tillich makes a great point about "being" and "nonbeing," both being within God and also that the divine darkness of God must be sought for. I wonder if it was really understood. I'm not active enough in theological circles to know; but it seems to me that if they had heard Tillich, they might have heard Jung, or if they heard Jung they might have heard Tillich. In any event, in my last conversation with Jung, I had the opportunity to talk with him about prayer. He said, And don't forget when you pray, above all else, bring your imperfections, because that's what God needs." It took me a while to understand that. We must bring our imperfections, because that's what God needs. Not only do I need to bring them, perhaps to be cleansed, to be purged, but also God needs them because there is a side of God that has never been incarnated in the Christian dogma. I believe that Jesus included both sides.

Jung also said that Self-understanding is precious not only to me but above all to the darkness of the creator who needs man, needs persons to illuminate his creation. We are needed to illuminate the darkness of the creator. I can only say that, as an analyst, there is probably no one problem that is harder for people to accept. It is one thing to say easily, "Of course I accept I have darkness, of course I accept that I sin—even perhaps that I am an awful sinner." One may sometimes take great pride in this. But it is another thing really to say to somebody, "I acted like a fool and I see where it came from and I'm really sorry I did it." That's accepting the darkness oneself.

Paul Tillich said that it is the good people who do the worst evil. I think Jung has helped us understand that profound statement. It is the "good" people who have, underneath their "good" side, so much that is not good. It is very hard for us to come to understand all-inclusiveness. In the synoptics, the statement, "You shall be perfect as your heavenly father is perfect" (Matt. 5:48) is better translated "You shall be all-inclusive." To be conscious of this part of me and of you, to be all-inclusive to myself—let alone to be able to be all-inclusive to other people—would mean we would be on the way to the Kingdom.

Most central, in terms of the contents of what is inside us, is the Self, this archetype of meaning which has become one-sided—has not contained all the opposites, and has become identified with the Christ figure. In being one-sided, rather than all-inclusive, the transforming power of the Self to reconcile opposites and to move to a new point is lost. Let me give you an example. A man whom I treated was very split between extreme hatred and hostility, and extreme tenderness and love. He was capable of both, but never the twain did meet. He could be very loving and tender and wonderful, and he could be simply horrible and full of hostility. And he went back and forth between these two. Not until he could accept both of them as part of the Self and of the God within could he find a way to reconcile them, to find a new point to integrate both of them, and to find a third point. It is one thing to go back and forth autonomously and never have them meet. But if a person can incorporate these two aspects of the Self, and has an ego to talk with, then something new can emerge that will be neither A nor B but their synthesis or third point.

In identifying the Self with the Christ, we have relied on a one-time incarnation rather than seeing incarnation as a continuous process, which perhaps both the God-process and we ourselves need. We have let Jesus carry the journey, forgetting that his life and growth are not helpful if we ignore this process in ourselves. Jung has written—and this may seem a theological point—that there is no Christ archetype. He said that a lot of people talk today about the Christ archetype. He says there can be a personification of the Self archetype in Jesus, but the trouble is then that the Self may become a matter of belief and not a matter of experience. Contrast this with Jesus, who related richly to his own inner processes in all of their dimensions. This touches a very deep subject, very inadequately, but I must leave it there.

What do we need today? Out of this brief survey, what *do* we need today? It is clear that we need the revitalization of traditional symbols and the creation of new symbols by individuals out of their own inner work. Only in this way can we break through the tightly bound symbols that have become dogmas. Even here there is danger within the Church. There is much of newness, it seems to me, from Church people with whom I work and who come to seminars. In the Church today, in terms of symbols such as liturgical dance, architecture, rearrangement of the structure of altars, the placing of the Eucharist, and so on, these represent a certain creative expansion. However, many people in the Churches are too concerned with "pepping up" their congregations. I use that crude word on purpose. Services become sort of a pep-up session, partly to get more members and more funds.

I may show my own position, but I'm quite willing to

stand on it. One may believe, because a rock mass is performed within a church, that in itself it becomes a new symbol. It could be. But it is also clear that it could be nothing but leaving people with a new outer form. Certainly, some of the masses done on the basis of the folk culture—Islamic, Missa Luba, Missa Pan Americana—fulfill a very different function. Some of the things that are going on in the church have to be judged as to whether they come under the heading of "newness." Do they really help to create new symbols that will lead us to inner richnesses? We need individuals who have the strength of commitment and dedication to open up the unconscious, but who also have the courage to work seriously in fantasy, in art of all kinds, in dreams, to help this inner world to become a spiritual source.

I began by saying we need to open up this depth, but we must also see what it wants. It desperately wants us as instruments, as organs, as tools who will express this. It is important to realize that real consciousness is not the same as to be conscious. Real consciousness will emerge only if there is a *confrontation with* the unconscious. Real consciousness emerges from the unconscious, or from the dialectic between conscious and unconscious. Real consciousness is not only our subjective feeling, but it also means being gripped by the dynamisms of the objective psyche, the archetype within us. I repeat this because there is a tremendous confusion between being concerned with our feelings—which is creative, but is not the same as really having knowledge—and coming to grips with and having a confrontation with the depths of the unconscious. We must not confuse feeling or thinking or any function with the contents of the unconscious.

If people work at this as individuals, it will have a tremendous influence on institutions, including the Church. I am interested in its possibilities. I have no idea of what the hope is for the Church. You will have to answer that question yourselves. But I am intensely interested in the possibility of individuals, ministers, priests, pastors, religious educators—all who work within the church, including laypeople—bringing new suggestions, new ideas as to what can happen. But this will only come about if the problem of the neglect of religious images is (in Tillich's terms) taken with ultimate concern as a neglect of God Him/Herself. The neglect of images and the neglect of symbols is the neglect of dealing with the divine. There are too many people today who flirt with the unconscious and have sort of a love affair with the unconscious. Everyone talks about Jung and the unconscious, but very few take it seriously.

Some of us, I hope, are going to take it seriously. Working with the unconscious is a matter of slow, patient work with inner and outer realities, of concern with inner realities and relating to our conscious historical situation. It is a task of helping that aspect of God become conscious, and of bringing the invisible into visible manifestation—in our life, our home, our family, our community, our church, our nation. Jung once said that there's no such thing as a self in a vacuum. We must live in the moment. We live in an existential reality. I am intensely concerned that existential reality needs to include the inner world, which is to be lived. The inner world is not the end in itself.

I would like to conclude with this: A couple of weeks ago, somebody made the following statement to me. I am not saying that I agree with it, but I pondered it, and then I decided to bring it here. He said he felt that in some of the theological seminaries there was a large amount of Christian Jungianism going on.

What did I think of it—Christian Jungianism?

In the first place, I don't think there is such a thing as "Jungianism." Jung would detest that phrase, just as Jesus would have some reaction to Christianity. Jung wasn't talking about an "ism." He was talking about a whole approach, a methodology if you will, but not an "ism." It is important to distinguish using Jung's method to understand and verify Christian symbols, that is, fitting Jung into Christian patterns without looking deeply at the implications—versus using Jung's approach to help us explore and critique Christian symbols and other symbols outside of Christianity in order to enlarge the area of understanding. This would not be to belittle it, but to find what may really be much richer than today's tradition. I think there's a danger that some of the Jungians and some of the theologians may be doing the first—using Jung's method to understand and verify dogmas and doctrines already held, versus the possibility of using this way of exploration to critique (and I'm using that in a very positive sense) some of these essentials of Christian symbols and dogma, to understand deeper truths that may be behind them.

The second seems to be what Jung was doing—to get at the deeper roots, which may then involve some major revisions of religious concepts. In the first, you hold the concept intact; in the second, you're willing to revise if it seems right. Not because Jung said it, but because his method helps to understand truths that have always been there. My own impression of Jung as a person was that he lived an enormous breadth and variety of symbols. Perhaps you have seen the movie which shows the stonework Jung created at Bollingen and the paintings he himself had done and the others which he had collected and displayed at his home at Kusnacht. And yet he always was rooted in his Western tradition. One had a sense, of course, that Jung knew the meanings inherent in the symbols. He did not stop with the symbols, he knew the meanings within them. They were part of him, and he also accepted his own limitation, as we all must. He knew his place in time and space with regard to the Other, and what the Other had asked of him during his years of life and what it needed of him.

I would like to end with something Jung said to me, and which has always delighted me. He said, "You know, we are but the spoons in God's kitchen." I think that Jung moved around his inner kitchen very deeply and dynamically, and it came to me this morning that as he moved around his inner kitchen he was always surprised at what he discovered there.

The Living Presences

"Praise to the affirmative angel."

"All angels are terrible."

These lines by the great mystical poet, Rainer Maria Rilke, express two seemingly contradictory qualities of one of the most persistent images in Western religion; the image of angels. Why so persistent? What do the angels symbolize of the eternal movements between human and God, in the universe and in the psyche?

Angelology is not my concern. I am concerned deeply, however, with the angel understood as an essential bridger of the chasm between our narrower self and the indwelling God of our deeper Self. Are we related to these angels as living presences, as they occur in Scripture, poetry, dream, myth? Or have the angels been killed, as have so many originally vital inner religious realities? Are we able to praise the "affirmative angels" of our lives, receiving all events, outer and inner, as bringers of messages from the divine, as helpers in the task of transformation? Are we able to understand and experience "all angels as terrible," *not because* they are negative, although they may look so, but because they express truths deeper than our self-centeredness can, and confront us with the need for new growth and flexibility? Are they terrible and awesome precisely *because* they are affirmative, carrying a power not subject to our egocentric will, but only to our willingness to listen to them? They ask questions; often they express the impossible possibility, thus they partake of the paradox of irrationality, of seemingly senseless things. When angels

* Presented at Grace Cathedral, San Francisco, California, January 28, 1973.

appear in myths, dreams, visions, they often have a knowledge of what is going on in the depths and heights of our inner world. They come in time of trouble, they bring wounding but also blessing. They suggest unforeseen developments.

How often do we say, without realizing what we say, "That must have been my guardian angel." Sometimes a certain situation recurs over and over in our life, and we neglect to read the signs as to why, especially with unpleasant situations. Dr. Fritz Kunkel spoke of the "archangels" as the purposive actors behind such occurrences, suggesting thereby some deeper reason than consciousness knows.

The angels connect us with the invisible world of religion and psychological meaning. In American Indian myth the winged messenger, by going between human beings and the gods, is in this sense angelic. In Egyptian mythology, a man talked with his Ba, his soul—or, putting it another way, he dialogued with an inner "angelical" eternal presence.

Such timeless events as these angels are among the more important experiences we average Christians are for the most part denied, because we have lost any viable relationship to their source in us. We are left lonely in a violent and destructive world. To rediscover our angels as richer resonances and patterns in our empty present requires us to work—yes, to work—at a conscious waking of fire in ourselves. The work must be conscious, or it will not serve God or man. We can no longer be unconscious about where things will come out. The terrible affirmative images will not, I hope, permit that unconsciousness.

In the Hebrew Scriptures reading of this service (Gen. 32:22-30), Jacob wrestles with a man (or Esau, his brother spirit—as his shadow), struggles with this mysterious dark adversary at the river's edge until dawn. His incredible statement to the angelic other was, "I will not let you go unless you bless me" (Gen. 22:26). Who among us is audacious enough, brave enough, to embrace the unknown challenge by asking its blessing? Jacob recognizes the importance of his adversary, knowing this angel of night contains healing power. He does not say, "I need to bless you

or accept you," albeit this may be included. He says, in effect, "I need to receive from you in the darkness what you
have to bring me, whatever that blessed gift is." It is as if
Jacob has to hold fiercely to the problems, difficulties,
adversaries, until that passionate consciousness wrests
from them what needs to be incorporated within ourselves.
The angel desires us and we the angel—this is the key to
the spirit's incarnation in human flesh. We must know and
act upon this mutual need, as Jacob did. Only such consciousness by a person—by you or me—can hold on at the
edge of night, despite wounds, can lift up a voice and be
answered. How many of us are willing to stay with our suffering until the suffering itself yields its healing? We would
rather flee to evasions of busy-ness, good works, anxiety,
and from them get the unhealing wound of incompleteness.

A somewhat similar situation is portrayed in the
modern religious play *Family Reunion*, by T.S. Eliot. In
this drama, the hero, Harry, has come back to his parental
home to face his problems and complexes, which are familiar to most of us. For years, Harry, away from the ancestral
home, has felt pursued by the fates—the Eumenides of
Greek myth. He feels they have pursued him, yet he daunt-
lessly struggles to have a confrontation with them, tries to
understand the meaning of his tormented journey to his
own individuality. When at last he faces them in the parental home and thus attains his freedom from them and is
ready to start forth on a new path, he says, "I must follow
the bright angels." The fearful, fateful problem becomes a
brighter destiny to be followed, becomes light through the
struggle with it. If we do not pursue such a course, our effort turns into flight and often into disaster.

In another Old Testament story (Num. 22:22-30),
Balaam, the prophet, has been ordered by Yahweh to per-
form a certain task. As he starts on his journey with his little ass, Yahweh sends an angel of the Lord to convey to
Balaam new instructions. Three times the angel bars the
way. Three times the little ass sees the angel and stops.
Balaam does *not* see and beats his beast for his behavior.
Yet she saves him from Yahweh's anger. The lower, instinctual part sees and hears, the well-adapted side not

only does not discern angels, but violently resents the little one who does. How often does our reasonable and well-indoctrinated side refuse to pay attention to little warnings and symptoms, small upsets that feel insignificant but that may express fuller purposes?

Finally, let us look at our Christmas myth and its angelic presences, and examine the differing attitudes of Zacharias and the shepherds upon receiving similar messages. Just as Jacob, Harry, Balaam, and his she-ass are each a part of our inner world, so also are Zacharias and the shepherds. Zacharias, the educated priest, father of John the Baptist, is told by the angel that he and his wife will indeed have a child, although his wife is long past childbearing age. Zacharias reacts with "What will be the sign?" (Luke 1:11-25). Because of his disbelief he is struck dumb by the angel until the birth comes about. Where, for us, does our disbelief in impossible potentials leave us stunted and mute? What Sören Kierkegaard called the "alarming possibility of being able" is not grasped by our Zacharias, although the angel attempted to say just that.

In contrast, the shepherds, like the simple and uncomplicated parts of us, when told by the angel of the New Birth, were "sore afraid" and sang praises. They responded—they trembled in the presence of the new—they took it as a Tremendum and were reverently fearful. They, in us, can fall to their knees before the Holy, whether the Holy is expressed in small or great events. The miracle of change and transformation of which the angels are constant reminders and mediators does go on between the Visible and Invisible, between our conscious side and our inner depths, between the known and the unknown, between time and the Eternal; the angelic presences are forever building bridges.

What can we say, then, of the purpose of angels? What is there for us, for our human side, to do? From these stories and many more, it seems the angels are purposive; their messages move us toward wholeness. They stand on the side of the evolutionary thrust of Teilhard's Omega point. They speak as voices of God, of that Other who forever calls, hoping a human being will respond, will enter

into dialogue. Of course we cannot know the exact relationship of the angel as Eternal Presence, as archetype of
meaning and wholeness to the Transcendent, the "God beyond God" in Paul Tillich's words. But it may be more than
a mere comfort to have some access to this God by way of
our interior numinous realm. Dr. Jung has said that the
angel personifies something new arising from the depth of
the unconscious. These depths have become available to
us again after a long absence. These religious depths await
response from us, unless we stay enclosed in our rigid personal, social, and theological systems.

Rilke has a beautiful line: "How tedious the angels
must find, lingering here." They wait patiently for response and we do not hear, do not answer. And the price of
our silence is a world of restless unhappiness. This darkness needs to be taken into each person's heart, struggled
with, and shaped into meaning.

In the wilderness experience of Jesus following the
Baptism, the Gospel of Mark states ". . . and he was with
the wild beasts; and the angels ministered unto him"
(Mark 1:13). The angels may be more intrinsically related
to the wild beasts then we have seen throughout our Christian history.

How may we help the angels emerge from the place
they have been put by our disbelief? How may we bring
them again into a joy full of pain and beauty? How help
enliven their energies through new forms of prayer, meditation, new ways of inclusiveness that will find a balance
between the I-Thou dialogue with the Transcendent in history and the danger of negative self-absorption? The Indwelling Presence as well as the divine coincidence of outer
events express these powers, called angels, who need to be
related to, not to be controlled or left unheard.

The "otherness" of the angels and at the same time
their interdependence with the human is lucidly stated by
W. H. Auden in the Christmas oratorio "For the Time Being." The angel speaks to Mary:

Today the unknown seeks the known,
What you willed to ask, your own
Will has to answer: child, it

lies within your power of choosing to
Conceive the child who chooses you.

The angels choose to speak God's will. Do we choose to accept or relate to their message?

Many of the traditional symbols in Scripture, creed,
and dogma need to express the vitality they *could* express
if all of us concerned with the Church would unite to help
this process. The angels and other symbols are not dead—
rather we have been cut off from our creative sources, and
the voice from the great Inner Silence. These can be recaptured with more knowledge of our own interior, where the
eternal truths flow, where the grace of God speaks through
such symbols as these angels.

Finally, let us ask ourselves these questions as we
prepare to bear new challenges from the angelic living
presences:

Have I seen the angels at work in darkest times?
Have I seen the angels at brightest times?
Have I opened myself to their messages?

Do I face these terrible but affirmative presences and,
most important, do I stay with them long enough to have
my life be the fulfillment it wants to be—needs to be—for
my sake and for the glory of God?

Darkness and God

Panel presented by Elizabeth Boyden Howes, Sheila Moon, and Luella Sibbald, and introduced by John Petroni

It is a rare opportunity to present this panel on darkness and God. A number of books have recently come out on the problem of darkness and evil and its relationship to God. Certainly it is a question that has agonized human beings for centuries. The panelists represent three varied and yet similar backgrounds, and we thought it would be very important for them to pool their ideas. They have worked for many years on the synoptic Gospels, both in individual study and in seminars with many different people. They all have backgrounds in analytical psychology, in which they have worked with individuals and also with themselves. They have taken in the whole area of mythology, their own journeys, and their own serious purposiveness, and they have looked at all this with courage and integrity, concerned about the larger purpose as it moves in the universe. So it seems a rare opportunity to bring them together to talk about this topic.

Elizabeth Howes: Notice the title of this panel, particularly what it is *not*. It is not called "Darkness in God," the "Origin of Darkness," the "Meaning of Darkness," the "Forms of Darkness," nor "Darkness and Evil." Rather it is called "Darkness and God." But perhaps the title raises the more ultimate question, the "why" of darkness. Why there at all? Why from the standpoint of the divine, and the why from the human standpoint? What does it say about

* Presented at the Guild for Psychological Studies, San Francisco, California, November 19, 1984.

the nature of things and about the nature of ourselves? We know from our Christian background that this is a difficult task, because of our prejudice against taking darkness seriously.

Dr. C. A. Meier, in his book *Ancient Incubation Rites and Modern Psychotherapy*, points out that those concerned with healing (we may not all be physicians, but we are all interested in healing), need also to be metaphysicians, people who can achieve a larger perspective regarding the process of transformation. It is to consider this larger perspective of being a metaphysician that we invite you to this panel tonight.

First, we will consider the forms and manifestations of darkness. Sheila Moon will speak to the Urgrund, the basic, ultimate, primal darkness out of which all things emerge. Luella Sibbald will present the beginning and evolution of opposites and polarities as the movement towards consciousness and the development of free choice; and I will present the forms and manifestations of darkness that we as humans need to face. Following this, each of us will present a brief summary on some of the meaning of darkness in its real unconsciousness. We will conclude by discussing what are the values and demands on us individually, to see the true facts as we have seen them, to achieve the perspective that is needed.

Sheila Moon: In virtually all beginnings of living things, there is darkness: the primal darkness, the Urgrund, or original depth, the primeval underground. Plants of virtually all kinds grow from seeds in the darkness under the earth, and have done so for millions of years. Most sea creatures of ancient times began in the deep darkness of sea fathoms. Great trees are rooted in the earth's depth; birds emerge from the darkness as their protecting egg-shell breaks open; animals, including humans, are long in the darkness of the womb. Also, animals have lived for millennia in deep and unlighted and protected cave darknesses, in the primal shelter where life can grow. Ancient humans also used deep caves for worship, as well as for birthing and comfort and often for art. The Urgrund, the original dark ground, is an ancient symbol related to many

of the great myths, and I want to touch on just a few, briefly, relating to the role of darkness in some of the ancient accounts.

The Urgrund was, and still is, a feature of myths of our
own continent, myths belonging to many Native American
tribes. Remember that myths are ways of describing how
events of nature and of humans struggle into consciousness. Even so small a thing as a seed falling into its
diminutive earthen darkness is life seeking its Urgrund.
Let us go far back in human history and examine the
nature of darkness as described by some of the leading
scholars throughout Europe.

Kerenyi describes the darkness of the ancient Greek
Mysteria Festival. He says that it is in three-fold darkness;
the darkness of the veiling, the darkness of the sacred
nights, and the darkness of one's own inner darkness, that
the seeker, man or woman, finds the way back to suffering
the motherliness, and at the same time the person is filled
with wonder at the eternal and common element in life's
beginning. So do individuals seeing origins in the persons
and destinies of the gods. Pindar, one of the earlier people
working with myth, has said that happy is the person who,
having beheld these things, descends beneath the earth.
The person then knows an end of a life, but also a God-
given beginning. In the Eleusinian Mysteries, there was
always darkness; the darkness of night, the darkness
before birth, the darkness of after-death, the darkness of
the cave—taken as a symbolic expression of a religious
feeling bound up with the earth. And indeed, in all primordial cults, we find the mysteries of birth, death, rebirth, ris-
ing from and returning to the darkness of the earth, where
it is shrouded and cared for in darkness. The Etruscan
Lamp, the alabaster bowl that reflected light—all these
things bear witness to the mysteries and extend beyond
Orphic mysteries and into the Christian world. Orphism
had quite an influence on the early Christian world and
also on our inner world. Hesiod of ancient Greece, in
describing the origin of humans, told of the chaos, void,
emptiness, as the beginning. Then came Gaia, Earth, and
the sequence of darkness, night, death and birth, sleep and
dreams. In Zoroaster's tradition, two of the greatest

gods—Ahuramazda, who was in the heights, and
Ahriman, who was in the deep darkness, and both were
both needed. So do we need them. Hesiod told that when
Kore was taken to the underworld by Pluto, the grain of
Demeter grew only part of the year out of the dark earth;
and in ancient Egypt, Osiris was raised from the underworld as grain. In both of these myths, darkness meant
growing.

I could take time to give some descriptions of some of
the ancient caves in Europe, but also in our Central
America, where natives have dwelled and painted and
carved on the walls the whole movement of the Urgrund
from the darkness to the light, and the gods, and the
various deities. This is very important to remember—that
this lives still in our land. The great world myths are not
fairy tales; they are true and religious descriptions of the
necessary dark and stillness made for growing, contain-
ment, awareness, and evolution. Certainly the God Presence is in this Urgrund in many ways. Children know this
when they explore darknesses and mysteries, or plant
seeds in dark ground and watch the green eventually rise.
We adults need to do this inwardly to learn the rich darkness of God.

Luella Sibbald: Out of the Urgrund, the primal darkness
found in all myths, there appears a natural need of movement toward differentiation into opposites and polarities.
Out of this emergence of opposites, without a doubt, conflicts, tensions, and aggressions occur, which result in the
inner and outer turmoil and chaos. Observation indicates
that this is the beginning of change and growth, which
seldom comes in any other way. If we go to our own creation myth in Genesis, we see this movement taking place.
The earth was without form and void, and darkness was
upon the face of the deep, and the spirit of God was moving
over the face of the waters. "And God said, 'Let there be
light'; and there was light. And God saw that the light was
good; and God separated the light from the darkness. God
called the light Day, and the darkness he called Night . . .
And God said, 'Let the waters under the heavens be

gathered together into one place, and let the dry land appear.' . . . God called the dry land Earth, and the waters that were gathered together he called Seas. And God saw that it was good." The emerging opposites were pleasing to God.

A very ancient myth speaks of Lilith. She was one. But the evolving process of birth to continue needed the opposites. It was too much for one. Lilith brought forth both Adam and Eve (male and female). Adam and Eve in unconsciousness were placed in the Garden of Eden, where God in two aspects of the deity resided as person and as serpent. In the garden of unconsciousness, or Paradise, two trees had been planted; one, the Tree of the Knowledge of Good and Evil, and the other, the Tree of Life. Adam and Eve were told by God that if they ate of the fruit of the Tree of the Knowledge of Good and Evil, that they would die. The serpent told Eve, "You will not die." Eve ate of the fruit of the forbidden tree and found it good, and gave some to Adam. Their act of eating brought them knowledge of their own nakedness and differentiation. The Kabbala says that man was created for the sake of choice. The eating of the Tree of the Knowledge of Good and Evil makes choice a necessity, for growth and consciousness as well as suffering.

The priority of movement toward opposites so far has been noticeably on the side related to the feminine; that is, the darkness, the water, the earth, Lilith, serpent, Eve, and even evil. The tree, with the roots in the feminine earth and its crown reaching skyward toward the masculine spirit, was a manifestation of the opposites needing to be united. The expulsion is carried out by God in His wrath, saying that, "If they should eat of the Tree of Life, they will be like one of us." The expulsion was done by God in the masculine aspect, which now begins to be more prominent than the feminine. Does God realize at this point that He needs humans to become conscious, and that He also needs consciousness—He needs consciousness—through deeper relationship with them? The expulsion, not Paradise, brings the possibility of consciousness to develop for God's creatures.

To eat from the Tree of Life is possible only when much growth is achieved. Each must consciously choose to enter the gate guarded by the cherubim with the flaming sword to reach the Tree of Life. This tree can be approached only by a person seeking individuation. This is just a beginning of the phenomenon of the opposites that must be integrated. Then the finding of the third point— that is, the journey back to the Tree of Life—may be achieved.

Elizabeth Howes: When we look at the basic Urgrund of being and the ultimate darkness out of which life and spirit begin to grow, and at the emergence of opposites and polarities wanting synthesis and solution, wanting to become conscious, it is not strange that the vehicle or instrument for that consciousness (a human being) will have from the beginning two levels of darkness to face. First there will be darkness itself, and then there will be the darkness of facing the darkness because of the freedom of will and the possibility of not facing it. Jung said that without freedom, individuation would be a senseless mechanism, worth neither thought nor effort. It would be fatality, not fulfillment. Conversely, it would lose all meaning if there were complete freedom, for it would then just go as well in one direction as another.

Jung, along with Jesus, and along with the great mystics, puts freedom of will at the center of being, at the center of the Self. So the new human instrument, then, faces overwhelming forces, both for ongoingness and progression and pull back and regression. What, then, are the forms or manifestations of darkness that the human being—you and I—must face?

The human faces the God/Yahweh/serpent ambivalence manifest everywhere, and faces all the opposites wanting integration that give rise to struggle, conflict, choice, and heroic achievement. In Deuteronomy 30:15 and 30:19, Yahweh says, "I have set before you life and good, death and evil, and again have placed blessing and curse; therefore, choose life, that you and your descendents may live." All myths of the journey to the Tree of Life show trials, tribulations, sufferings, along with joy. How could this not be true, if the human is to face the ambivalence in God and the opposites of the archetypes that need integration? Courage and will are needed for the newcomer in the evolutionary scale, to break loose from the shackles of the bondage of instinct, habit, and collective pattern. Again, Jung has said that will is energy, freely disposable by the psyche, as opposed to energy chained to the instincts and the autonomous complexes. The challenge is what we do with this will.

We see, in all the stories of the journey, the shadow in its negative sense of pulling us away from central intentionality. As has been said, God is that freedom that must be used creatively in choice for value-centeredness. God alone cannot, does not, control His/Her irrational side, along with all the other qualities of the deity, but needs a human to bring this to consciousness. Again, we experience loss, tragedy, sorrow—sometimes from our own egocentricity, sometimes from happenings not of our own doing. Constantly we meet unanticipated events that present grave problems of acceptance and choice. The words of Job 2:10 confront us: "If I receive good from God, why should I not receive evil?" (Or what sometimes feels like evil.) From these forms of darkness—ambivalences, opposites, complexities in our own nature, losses and tragedies in outer and inner events—there is suffering. This suffering is uncreative and meaningless if seen only from an egocentric point of view. It is creative if we allow it to move us to a deeper reality and value.

Do we see that we are here to serve and not to be served, to help God/value become, and not to pretend that we are owners of the universe?

We also see sheer, unadulterated evil in the inner and outer world—things that people do out of the unattended libido that goes off autonomously, without direction. Here the darkest elements in the psyche express themselves. Reflecting that we are made in the image of God, we may say the elements that are present in God and Self as we saw them in the Tree of the Knowledge of Good and Evil are the ones that most need transformation to save the world and ourselves, and perhaps the divine itself. The forms of these are well known: power, hostility, aggression, racism, destroying the earth, hatred, violence, and so forth.

And finally, there is a darkness of death, physical death, which brings the death/rebirth archetype into its final movement for each individual. Do we accept this? Do we let go to it, whatever our age? The Chinese say the greatest good fortune a man can meet is to find the death that crowns his life—his own specific death. All these different forms of darkness that the human must meet—ambivalences, opposites, suffering, losses, tragedies, evil, death—are so varied; but they are there and must be met by each of us, so that the hidden goal that drives for fulfillment has a chance to come to birth. Without meeting them, there is no chance for this birth.

These, then, are the forms and manifestations of darkness. Now, each of us will try to formulate briefly something of our own understanding of the meaning of these truths and their implications.

Sheila Moon: I am going to be touching again on some of the native American myths which, despite their primitiveness, are incredibly rich with movements that each of us can profit from in the kind of moving that Elizabeth Howes was just talking about.

As I said earlier, a child learns not to fear the dark if adults have explored their own darkness and its God source. I say this again, because I've seen it. A child learns not to fear the dark if adults have explored their own darkness and its God source. Much the same can be said about animals. Both children and animals, before long, do find darkness fearful, but they are also excited with the mystery to be searched for. I wonder how many of us are able to face the darkness and its mystery and get excited about searching for what is really in it of its own God nature. I suggest that you try it some time, and maybe sit with a child or an animal.

Kore was taken to the underworld, as I said earlier, by the god of darkness, Pluto; but Demeter's grain continued to grow even if it took it half a year to do so. But it did grow. If life, as Kore, is deliberately put down in us, we are in a dark time. This is why this myth is effective. If we can see

that despite the fact that Kore was taken to the underworld, to the Urgrund, she was able to face the dark time
and come through it, we can do likewise—if we work with
it. As in the myth, the answer is that the growth of the goddess inside must be aided. The grain as seed is in the
Urgrund, and it must be tended in light as well as in
darkness.

The emergence myth of the Navajo is, as I see it, a won-
drous telling of starting in the Urgrund and slowly and
with difficulty making a climb from unconsciousness to a
place where conscious growth begins, and where new
levels in growing awareness proceed. Some of you know
this myth, about which I have written in *A Magic Dwells*. It
is very important to see the movement in that myth—the
movement up from the darkness, and the people beginning
to feel something else has to happen. They begin to move,
and they forget things, and that's when they get Pot Carrier, the little beetle, to go back and get the things they
forgot. If we can permit ourselves to take this attitude,
there is a great movement from our dark place to a place
where the dark becomes meaningful and something new
happens. It must never be forgotten that we are far more
than consciousness—we are our darkness, also. We are beings with a magnitude of unconscious dimensions and
levels forever at work in us. What we need is to find the
Urgrund in ourselves and the unconscious "others" inside.
If we descend to the Urgrund and come face to face with
the dark unknown, we also face God. Psychological and religious redemption are the acts of recovering for ourselves,
out of the dark beginning, values which we know are our
own, but which we also know we have lost. In the darkness
of Urgrund we find values we can now retrieve, in the same
way that Pot Carrier beetle does in the Navajo emergence
myth. He brought them up. It is this "small" in us (and by
"small," I'm not talking about unimportant or insignificant; I'm talking about the diminutives in us that we walk
away from all the time) that can, over and over again,
climb up to consciousness out of the darkness and recover
our God/Self.

Another example, from a Pima myth: In the beginning,
there was only darkness everywhere, darkness and water.

And the darkness gathered thick, crowding and separating, until at last out of a crowded darkness a human came. It wandered the darkness until it began to be conscious, and then it knew it was human and was there for some purpose. This is a very important thing for every one of us to remember—what it would be like to know we were human, and that where we are, whatever the struggle is, we are there for some purpose. So this also describes how human consciousness must work, through the needed darkness of God, in order to come face to face with that God who is in us and in our outer being. It may not be consciousness as we know it in our first choices, but somehow, some dim sense of meaning, some impulse in us forms for an upward thrust. We do not know who or what makes the decision, but it is made. Choice seems to be there from the beginning. When in myths, as creator, God is present, the choice is more clearly formulated. Even when a creator God is not there, however, in myths such as the Navajo, choices are made. With little Pot Carrier beetle's help, the people are pushed upward. The creator God is there as a symbol of our will to live.

Luella Sibbald: The process of God is freedom and development. What does reality say to us that comes from the implication development of God's freedom in us? One reality that needs serious consideration is the fact of the four elements: earth, water, air, fire. The first three are intimately related to animal life. Many forms of animal life are found in each element, the land, the seas, and the air. Some animals move in only one element, others are at home in two, and fewer can move in all three elements.

No animal can relate to fire. Only a person can deal with it, both in its destructive and transformative states. The myth tells us that Prometheus stole a brand of holy fire from the immortal forges, to bring it to earth. He risked the freedom he had to give mortals this element of powerful force, with implications in both its opposites. The wrath of Zeus was great. Prometheus, as a result, was chained to a rock with indestructible chains. An eagle fed on his liver. As much as was eaten each day grew back each night. Thirty years of this suffering was endured when he was rescued by Hercules, who slew the eagle and broke the chains. Some compromises were made with the gods, and Prometheus was allowed to join the immortals again. However, to risk the freedom given to upset the plan of the gods can be a serious, suffering situation.

Fire, on the postive side, is crucial to humankind. Outwardly we use it for light or warmth, or to prepare nourishment. Inwardly, it is related to our vitality for life, our passion in life, and our will, especially the will to do the will of God. Negatively, it is a tremendously destructive element when loosened for that purpose. This is our situation now, being unconscious in our apathy to let things happen. Or is there the consciousness in the world to shape things differently, that there may be a new covenant with God, so that the beauty of the planet and the evolutionary process in individuals can go on?

The element that is uppermost in each age demands certain forward changes in growth. The evolutionary step that this air age makes possible, as well as asking its development for our own survival, is that each person find his/her centeredness. Air does not lend itself to perceptual boundaries. Without a well-established centeredness in our own being, related to the ego-Self axis, one can be tossed hither and yonder, and mental disorientation and difficulties can be more easily manifested in an air age. I think we are aware of that in many ways right now. Erich Neumann said that once we have understood that the ego can never exist and develop without the Self that underlies it, we arrive at the crucial Copernican revolution of depth psychology which views the human personality and human life no longer from the standpoint of the ego, but from that of the Self, around which the ego revolves. One world with a world center is a necessary movement in this approaching millennium.

Elizabeth Howes: You and I are faced with the darkness that is creative because it is the womb out of which light and consciousness comes, the darkness that is painful but necessary to bring integration out of the opposites and to appease the hunger and longing of that which wants integration, and whose wrath in many forms is aroused if not fulfilled. We must travel to the interior to meet the outer, where opposites express themselves in history. We must journey to the interior because it is finally the source, the place where healing of splits and conflicts takes place. Only we as humans can reflect, interpret, and act, so that freedom which is God becomes creative and not negative. As Kazantzakis has said, the universe is imperiled by our sloth, our lethargy, and our unconsciousness.

Two recent historical events bear witness to this only too dramatically: the election in our country, and the assassination of Indira Ghandi. Both of these events—the election of a conservative and unprepared leader for threatening global problems, and the gunshot killing of a very creative feminine woman—are examples of what can destroy our planet. The forces and the dynamisms of the opposites are so very strong, and the thread—the tiny, delicate but indestructible and indispensable thread of God's meaning—is so small, yet everything hangs on it. This may be called the Holy Spirit at work. The darkness of the split-off power inside us, projected into the outer world, and the resultant wrath of God if we don't deal with these realities, is ever-present. This wrath takes on the form of apocalypticism, where all hope is projected into a future redeemer, and the present is left in despair. Its opposite, the grace and love of God, is there if we do act. These are hard darknesses to face, as different from the darknesses of the creative Urgrund. However, they are interrelated, and both are central to our existence and to our consciousness.

The suffering to actualize the journey in myself, to being into the real world fulfillment of God's need and mine, is balanced by the joy of knowing one is at the heart of things, at the core of meaning and fulfillment, whether this is expressed in the Yakima Indian story of the hazelnut which many of us know, in the Navajo emergence, in finding the Tree of Life, or in moving into the Kingdom of God.

Now, finally, what does it demand of us, to attempt to see things with this kind of perspective?

Sheila Moon: The human task, at this juncture of our history, is to climb again out of our contemporary Urgrund—the terrible darkness of nuclear weapons, and the other darknesses of starving humans, of losses of lands and wildlife because of human greed. If we could and would leave this behind, we would radically become humans of open religious consciousness. Jung said that things reaching so far back into human history naturally touch upon the deepest layers of the unconscious, and can have a powerful effect upon it, even when our conscious language proves itself to be quite impotent. Such things cannot be thought up, but must grow again from the forgotten depths, if they are to express the supreme insights of consciousness and the loftiest intuitions of the spirit, and in this way fuse the uniqueness of present-day consciousness with the age-old past of life.

Jesus and many of the great mystics in one way or another considered God as freedom in our deepest Self. Let us remember that. We must climb again out of our contemporary Urgrund, and open ourselves to a deeper religious consciousness. Maeterlinck, one of the great naturalists, said about fifty years ago that it comes to pass with bees, as with most of the things in this world, we remark some of their habits and imagine we know them, but if we draw near, we are confronted by the enigma of intellect, destiny, will, aim, means, causes, the incomprehensible organization of the most insignificant act of life. I would like to repeat this because to me it is very moving, articulating Maeterlinck's relationship to bees as tiny little creatures that seem to not belong to anything or anybody, and if we can see what he is saying here about the human. He says that it comes to pass with bees, as with most of the things in this world, we remark some of their habits and imagine we know them. Parenthetically I would say this is what we do with ourselves, one of the things in this world: We mark some of our habits and imagine we know them, and we know where the world is going, of course. Obviously, it is all very clear. But if we draw near, we are confronted by the enigma of intellect, destiny, will, aim, means, causes. And if you can say that to yourself and to our fellow humans, can we confront ourselves and others with the enigma of intellect, destiny, will, aim, means, causes? If we did that, we would be in a much better position than we are today.

We would stand in awe before the incomprehensible
organization of the most insignificant act of life.

There may not be consciousness as we know it in these
choices to descend into the unknown Urgrund of God. We
do not know who or what makes the final decision. Something knows. When in the great myths a creator god is
present, the choice is clear; for the creator God is at bottom
a symbol of our will to live. Yahweh said to Noah (Gen.
9:13-16), "Whenever I bring clouds over the earth, a rainbow will appear in the clouds, and then I will remember
my covenant between myself and you." When the rainbow
appears in the clouds, I will see it, and remember the
everlasting covenant between Yahweh and every living
creature of every sort that is on the earth—including us.

And God moves from fruitful darkness in us to our full
and luminous consciousness if we do our part in our emergence. The eternal flow of life can continue only through a
recurrent sacrifice by way of death, rebirth, and holding
God's needs and human needs together.

Luella Sibbald: What is demanded of us? In the areas that
we have emphasized, in the need of the opposites and the
elements, the conscious awareness of the dark side of the
opposites, or the darkness that may come from lack of
awareness of the elements, one is dealing with needs to be
honored as part of the whole. If we follow the words of
Jesus, and resist not evil, then the dark, satanic, evil side
in each of us must be accepted, related to, and integrated
with the light side, to find the new emerging objectivity of
the third point. Sometimes a radical outlook needs a new
attitude in expressing integrity in ethical questions. Our
whole way of thinking has to be questioned and altered, to
envision what is needed. We easily overlook the basic
needs in changing our way of perceiving life.

One of these incidents of change could be in how we
value the guilty person, how neglectful of really consider-
ing them we are. Why did God mark Cain's forehead so he
would not be killed, although he had killed his brother,
Abel? This kind of consciousness is the kind that can
emerge only when relatedness to the unconscious is present. Jung has said, in *Answer to Job,* that the guilty man is

eminently suitable and therefore chosen to become the vessel for the continuing incarnation, not the one who holds aloof from the world and refuses to pay his tribute to life, for in him the dark God would find no room. Jung said further that the incarnation has to be in the dark God, and not in the light God. Therein lies the value of the guilty person, for this opposite has been completely ignored. Another time, Jung asked a friend if he had ever heard the parable of the unjust steward. The friend said he hadn't. Jung indicated that theologians never preach about that, for Jesus praised the man who had cheated, or in other words, the man who was fully conscious. This man was fully aware of both opposites, so, to repeat the words that are very familiar, "Blessed art thou if thou know what thou doest, and cursed art thou, and a transgressor of the law, if thou knowest not."

Elizabeth Howes: What is demanded of us? It demands courage—deep, hardcore courage of a committed ego, and ego/Self/God affirmation. It needs understanding and reflection on the why of darkness, as we have tried to put it this evening. This means objectivity—as separate, often, from our Christian prejudice. It means an understanding of the nature of the psyche and the symbolic life, and the need and role of symbols to work with darkness. It is obviously beyond the scope of this panel tonight to talk of how to work with all the forms of darkness.

Yes, it demands working through our own rigidities, and to come to new ways of knowing, not just with our heads, but with our heart coming into soul knowledge. It demands prayer, the kind of prayer that Jung refers to as that which makes the beyond we conjecture and think about an immediate reality, and transposes us to the duality of the ego and the dark other. Jung then points out that the question arises, What will become of the transcendent Thou and the immanent I?

It may not be inappropriate to end by saying that we each need to find our own answer to God, as Jesus found his. We have really tonight defined God, not in an abstract way, but as the ever-emergent mystery from deepest depth to the height of fulfillment.

Opposites: Divided or Reconciled?

In the beginning there was singular oneness, complete but motionless. The *unus mundus*—one world—it has been called. All parts are present but undifferentiated. This one world holds the core of our creation and of possible emergence. Seemingly still it rests, but somewhere inside a fire burns, a pulse beats, a center yearns to become something more. It has been called a garden, with the Tree of the Knowledge of Good and Evil, and the Tree of Life. In Jewish mysticism it is called the Sephiroth Tree. An ancient Gnostic text expresses it thus:

> In the beginning, before the world was,
> I and Thou are one.
> Thou before me;
> I the one who comes after you.
> This power is one.
> It separated itself towards above and below.
> It is its own mother and its own father.

Whatever it is called, it is not static but dynamic, whether describing the beginning of the cosmos or the beginning of the world inside each of us. It is filled with longing for its parts to become related and to know one another. It wants to know itself, and the opposites which are there.

In the book of Isaiah (45:7) the One says: "I form light and create darkness." In the ancient Mayan myths, the Maker and the Heart of Heaven brood under blue and green feathers, deciding what is to become. The masculine and the feminine are always there as bivalences between light and dark, above and below, left and right. These opposites must be acutalized by complementing one another, by

---

* Presented at First Unitarian Church, San Francisco, California, April 23, 1979, under the auspices of the Guild for Psychological Studies.

working together and thus moving forward. Life must be movement and change, not stasis. Complementarity is always at the base of life and of true creativity. This longing for a dynamic interrelation between parts cannot be fulfilled by the One alone, the lonely deity. There must be a choicemaker to break stasis and to help the One achieve new unity and needed growth. So opposites are realities, and interaction between them is necessary for the fire of consciousness within the One to become a reality. The human is needed for the evolving growth urgent in the outer world as well as in the inner world. The Other cannot be creative alone, nor can the human. The Other, and the human with Self-ego, are both essential.

Each opposite to be faced and dealt with in the combined work of God-human can become—and usually does become—a kingdom of its own, capable of autonomous action, forgetful of the existence of all other realities. This separation between opposites becomes a wound in both God and the human psyche, and the wound can only be healed by the co-creative work toward unification.

How specifically can these wounds be healed? What must each side—human and God—contribute for a new reconciliation, a greater wholeness, wherein the One becomes unified more fully with the addition of human consciousness? We must be aware of what the human brings and what God brings. The beginning becomes always now as the task of the achievement of integration of opposites—expressing the desire of God's becoming. It is to go forward, not by leaving the opposites behind or by transcending them altogether, but by transforming them through the discovery of new reconciliations. Our planet's life and our individual lives may be determined by how we meet this challenge. We have oneness with parts, and a sense of desire for becoming. We have opposites created within the whole, but unintegrated. We do also have human creation in co-creation with the divine, and it helps the potential become actual and incarnate if we are responsible.

What I have just said as introduction is a desire to state my understanding and vision of this myth and meaning of the Western world. I will describe the five fullnesses—oneness, opposites within it, bringing human creativity into Life, the autonomy of the opposites, and finally the work of co-creation. These concepts need to be enfleshed with full human understanding if they are to become life-giving.

In the Garden of Eden there is the Lord God, and there is the serpent, created by the Lord God, each expressing opposite points of view. There is ambivalence about the desire for consciousness, but the serpent does win and Paradise is broken out of its static state. Thus true consciousness begins. The Garden contains the knowledge of good and evil and the Tree of Life. Light and dark are there. Choice is there. Masculine and feminine are there, expressed when humans are created "in our image," as God said (Gen. 1:26). Spirit and substance are there. All these polarities are within the one Garden.

Dr. Jung has said that polarity means a potential. And where potential exists, there is a possibility of a current, a flow of events, a tension of opposites striving for balance. To see these opposites as antinomies within God is to dignify our own personal struggles with them. And our struggles with them are very great in order to discover the third point, the reconciling transcendent symbol beyond them.

The most central pair of opposites, which I have not yet mentioned within the Godhead, are love and wrath. We see these expressed in both the Hebrew Scriptures and in the New Testament, or in the great prayer from the Jewish Midrash, where God prays: "May it be by will that my mercy may suppress my anger and my compassion may prevail over my other attributes." This is the heart-cry of God, longing for the triumph of love from His/Her core into ours. He/She says in it, "May it be my will."

What must the human be like to meet the demands of unifying such very great opposites? If the human is to be like God, what must be encompassed? The ambivalence within God will surely be reflected in the ambivalence within God's most secret dwelling place in the human psyche, in the Self. The Self has within it progressive and regressive elements, but it also has a pinpoint of desire to be on the side of creation rather than on the side of destruction. In the human, the opposites are expressed in the archetypes, of which Jung says that the archetypes are not static, but in continuous flux. There is no energy without opposites and the Self will hold the potential healing symbol whose power will bring the unification.

Out of the Self there must be an emergent ego, something rooted deep down, with freedom to say yes and no. In fact, freedom is the chief characteristic of God. There must be the choicemaker. This capacity for yes and no, with a Yes beyond to both, is described eloquently by the great theologian Paul Tillich. We also find it in Jung's statement where he writes that the dualities of yes and no are at bottom the irreconcilable opposites, but they have to be held together if the balance of life is to be maintained. This can only be done by holding unswervingly to the center where action and suffering balance each other.

This choiceful factor could be called the fourth point, because it determines how the work of integration proceeds. Jung states that the unconscious consists of opposites, and a moment will come when the individual must hold fast so as not to be thrown catastrophically off balance. The holding fast can be achieved only by a conscious will, the ego. That is the great and ineffable significance of the ego.

Coming closer to where we are now existentially, why is it that some opposites are much harder for Christians to face than others? Our one-sided theology is too often based on a misunderstanding of total truth of mythological and psychic facts. We praise and laud partial aspects of God, not God in His/Her unfathomable, awesome, glorious, and terrifying reality. What is most praised in our culture? Spirit, not substance; masculine, not feminine; light, not dark, in the sense of down and in; good, not its opposite, evil; perfection, not imperfection; extraversion, not introversion; rational, not irrational; and many more could be added to that. Most especially, perhaps, do we need to see our refusal to face evil, inner and outer. Trusting it only as a diminution of good—the *privatio boni*—is to discount the forceful power of evil and of wrath, which is so rampant in the world today because we haven't faced it.

What does this one-sidedness do to us as individuals? And how is it reflected in our social structure? We are split and we live in a split world, each opposite defending its own corner and passionately believing "God is on our side." It is a world where white power represses dark minorities; where extravert achievement is put above inner individual development. All "isms" have about them the danger that they will run rampant and catch the ego so powerfully that all perspective is lost. What is demanded of the ego is that it should become free from identification with any one parital one-sidedness or any collective goal. Erich Neumann, in his book *Depth Psychology and a New Ethic*, speaks of the old ethic being the Judaic-Christian ethic of one-sidedness, and the new as being all-inclusiveness. He writes: "The ultimate aspiration of the old ethic was partition and dichotomy, as formulated in the mythological projection of the Last Judgement, under the image of the separation of the sheep from the goats. The ideal of the new ethic is a combination of opposites into a unitary state." To help society (and myself) bring about this unitary structure I must, according to Dr. Jung, surrender to a power beyond the opposites, to a superior divine factor.

Finally, then, where does reconciliation lie? Dr. Jung has said that reconciling symbols come through the Holy Spirit working in the unconscious in dreams and in visions; for in the Holy Spirit the opposites are no longer separated. I would like to add two points to this. There can be no reconciling and healing symbol unless there is a person to receive the power behind the symbol and to let the gift enter and be worked with consciously. We must be aware that reconciling symbols come in many ways other than dreams—sudden outer experiences, meeting people, situations, synchronicities. For example, one may be struggling with two directions of doing or saying something that is a particularly important confrontation. It could be said in a way which one knows is a more feminine way or in a more masculine way—regardless of whether we are men or women. Something, perhaps, happens—we meet someone, we hear a piece of music—something happens that forms a healing symbol from the outside and brings a wholly new perspective for action. This kind of healing happens all the time if we are alert to watch for the purposiveness of these healing symbols as they appear.

The enumeration of healing symbols would be extensive. Sometimes they are found in traditional religious symbols—the child, the hermaphrodite, the rose, the Star of David, mandalas, pieces of music. I want to read in a condensed form the magnificent vision found in Ezekiel. I see this as a very great example of a healing symbol. Jung has said that it is one of the great healing symbols in the form of spoken mandala. (Those of you who know Ezekiel far better than I may feel I have left out the most important sentence.)

> . . . behold, a stormy wind came out of the north, and a great cloud, with brightness round about it, and fire flashing forth . . . and . . . the likeness of four living creatures . . . each had four faces, and . . . four wings . . . the face of a man . . . the face of a lion . . . the face of an ox . . . the face of an eagle . . . And each went, without turning as they went. In the midst of the living creatures there was something that looked like burning coals of fire . . . and the fire was bright . . . There were wheels beside the living creatures, on the earth, one for each one. They had rims and eyes. There were wheels within a big wheel. Wherever the living creatures went, they went.
>
> Over the heads of the living creatures there was the likeness of a firmament, shining like crystal, over their heads there was the likeness of a throne, in appearance like sapphire; and seated above the likeness of a throne was a likeness as it were of a human form. And upward from what had the appearance of his loins I saw as it were gleaming bronze, like the appearance of fire enclosed round about; and downward from what had the appearance of his loins I saw as it were the appearance of fire, and there was brightness round about him. Like the appearance of the bow that is in the cloud on the day of rain, so was the appearance of the brightness round about.
>
> Such was the appearance of the likeness of the glory of the Lord. And when I saw it, I fell upon my face, and I heard the voice of one speaking.
>
> And he said to me, "Son of man, stand upon your feet, and I will speak with you." (Ezekiel 1:4-28)

I chose this in part because I think sometimes we have lost in our literature, biblical and other traditions, some of the marvelous symbols that are there and which we could well use for work.

The work with these healing symbols—great or small—might freshly be called "integrative mysticism." I am adding this phrase (I have never come across it) to Martin Buber's classification of the mysticism of absorption and identification, which he says is more Eastern, and the mysticism of relationship—the I-Thou—which is especially described in the Judaic-Christian tradition. Integrative mysticism might be understood as the mysticism of integration, where the mystical act is a more total act of receiving the depth within the symbol, but with the knowledge one has of one's own psyche, letting the opposites be invaded by that central reality. The moving image of the rainbow may come in a dream. Is the ego present to let it permeate the consciousness fully and to work there to bring the disconnected parts of the psyche into its healing influence? The fire of God, longing to become, becomes available to the Self when an ego is present to carry it and to help it permeate the whole. Perhaps one of the great dangers of religious experience, and even of certain types of mystical experience, is the danger of their being cut off from the rest of the psyche instead of permeating and imbuing the rest of the psyche with meaning.

How has this revelation of reconciliation through the Holy Spirit come about in our tradition? If one moves beyond the Christian tradition to its source, one comes to understand several things about the partialness of the Christian approach. As it is described in the gospels, Jesus experienced the descent of the Holy Spirit as a dove, marking God's desire to come closer to the human. This Holy Spirit drove Jesus to the wilderness, to face the conflicts that Satan presented, and later became Jesus' teacher, the source of what to say at times of crisis—surely a reconciling symbol. The whole life of Jesus was one of facing opposites and, finally, during the ultimately reconciling act of being willing to be killed, to bring the two sides of God—the wrath and the love—together. The love and the wrath and their intersection is perhaps what is meant by the symbol of the cross, with the human, or the human in me, on it.

I would like to paraphrase one of Dr. Jung's letters on what we have done with the cross and why. It is one of his more forceful letters.

Christ forces man into the impossible conflict. He took himself with exemplary seriousness and lived his life to the bitter end, regardless of human convention and in opposition to his own lawful tradition, as the worst heretic in the eyes of the Jews and a madman in the eyes of his family. But we? We imitate Christ and hope he will deliver us from our own fate. Like little lambs we follow the shepherd, naturally to good pastures. No talk at all of uniting our Above and Below! On the contrary, Christ and *his* cross deliver us from our conflict, which we simply leave alone. We place ourselves under *his* cross, but by golly not under our own. To put oneself under somebody else's cross, which has already been carried by him, is certainly easier than to carry your own cross amid the mockery and contempt of the world. That way you remain nicely ensconced in tradition and are praised as devout.

So the end becomes the beginning again. The task is to stand in the midst of our inner and outer world with all of its splits, its apocalyptic divisions keeping good and evil separated, and thus staying in safe little compartments. But we can do otherwise, if we take up the process creatively in full knowledge that behind the opposites something, somebody, some reality is operative, longing to give the gift of reconciliation if there are receivers. The numinosity of the divine is lost for actualization without persons as receivers, with courage and Self-knowledge, and openness to the manifestation of the Spirit out of substance. With no person to carry the solutions, the planet remains sterile. There are gifts and there is grace, but the work is ours and it is not child's play. But through psychological work, active imagination, meditation and prayer, the center of love beyond all opposites is revealed and God's magnet pulls us to reconciliation. Then we may face the flaming sword and the Cherubim and return to eat of the Tree of Life and perhaps to make all things new and beautiful.

INDEX

at Baptism of Jesus, 19, 20, 49,
58-60, 64-65
blasphemy against, 61-62
as connective between divine
and human, 4
and Crucifixion, 62-63
in Hebrew Scripture, 54-57
and incarnation, 61, 64
as Paraclete, 64
and Pentecost experience, 22
predominates in new (Aquarian)
age, 19, 53
as reconciler, 53, 57, 59, 61,
127, 129
and substance, 65
as teacher of what needs to be
said, 62
and threatened destruction of
planet, 118
human, God's need for
for co-creation, 87, 124
for consciousness, 3, 73, 90, 98,
113, 124
for fulfillment of Kingdom, 16
to illuminate God's darkness, 95
for incarnation, 14, 72, 95
to integrate God's opposites,
3, 13, 20, 55, 124
for mercy and love, 35
humanization, 28
Huxley, Aldous, 1

I

I AM, 52, 58
images, religious, 89-99
neglect of, as neglect of God, 98
see also symbols, religious
imago Dei
at descent of Holy Spirit, 59
perceived in enemy, 28
Self as, 4, 71, 91
incarnation
angels and, 103
contemporary lack of relation
to, 80-81
in dark side of God, 121
God's need of human for, 14,
72, 95

and guilty person, 121
Holy Spirit and, 61, 64
from inner world of psyche,
90-91
Jesus' *vs.* others', 19, 33
represented in Mass, 82
see also child, divine
incarnational theology, 30, 31, 33,
34, 42
inclusiveness
ethic of, 78, 127
of Jesus, 10-11, 20-21, 95
perfection as, 10, 95
individuation, 10, 70, 77, 80
freedom required for, 112
represented in Mass, 81

J

Jacob (patriarch), 102-3
Jaffe, Aniela, 72
Jeremiah (prophet), 57
Jerome, Saint, 62
Jesus of Nazareth
Baptism experience of, 4, 17-19,
20, 29, 49, 58-60, 64-65, 129
on broad and strait way, 1
and Christ-consciousness, 4, 19,
82; as projected by others, 9,
9, 19-20
conscious relation to, 9
Crucifixion of, 62-63, 80-81
and darkness, 62-63, 80-81
and/on evil, 10-11; see also
"resist no evil"
inclusiveness of, 10-11, 20-21, 95
and/on Kingdom of God, 15, 16
myth and history and, 45-52
his myth *vs.* Christian myth, 2,
19-20, 22, 46-47
as object of worship and carrier
of others' journey, 8-9, 10, 21,
50-51, 80, 96;
Jung on 8-9, 12, 50, 71, 129
parables of, 16-17, 121
Resurrection of, 49
Sonship of, 49, 50, 59-60, 65
Joachim de Flore, 19, 53

Job (in Hebrew Scripture), 18, 56,
94, 113
John the Baptist, 16, 20, 58
journey, psychological, 91
Jesus as carrier of, 8, 96
perseverence in, 72
shadow and, 113
Jung, Carl Gustav, 67-73
on angels, 105
Answer to Job, 120-21
author and, 67-68, 71-72, 73, 99
on Christ image, 20, 77, 78;
as archetype, 9a6
dangers in psychology of, 72
on dogma and Church, 9-10
on evil, 10, 11
and Freud, 68, 69, 90-91
on God, 20, 69; as different
from God image, 77; as different from Self, 4, 71, 91;
on God's need for human, 13,
72, 73, 90, 94-95; opposites
in, 13, 53, 65; as "too light,"
93
on Holy Spirit, 53
on imitation of Christ, 8-9, 12,
21, 50, 130
letter to a minister, 12, 21
50, 129-30
on Mass, 81, 82
Memories, Dreams, Relfections,
70, 90; dreams in, 68-69
on prayer, 71-72, 94-95
Psychology and Religion, 76,
82, 83
religious concern of, 70-72, 76,
90
resistance to, 67, 70, 71
Secret of the Golden Flower, 8-9
Seven Sermons to the Dead, 70
on symbols, 12, 71
on Trinity, 59, 63
on willpower, 6, 73
Jung, Emma, 67, 72
"Jungianism, Christian," 98-99
Justin Martyr, 59

K

Kazantzakis, Nikos, 2, 118
Kerenyi, Karl, 109
Kierkegaard, Soren, 104
Kingdom of God
Jesus and/on, 15, 16
parables on, 16-17
and Third World, 23, 27, 29-30,
34, 35-38
"within/among you," 4, 17,
18-19, 29
Klausner, Joseph, 18
Kore and Demeter, 110, 114-15
Kunkel, Fritz, 102

L

Lamb of God, 50
liberation, in Third World, 25-28
theology of, 31, 32, 33
light and dark
Christianity and, 10
in creation myth (Genesis),
110-11
within God, 10, 18, 20, 56
split between, 10, 12
symbolized in Cross, 80
see also darkness
Lilith, 111
liturgy
as container of archetypes, 75
Euchrist, 81-84
Jung and, 71
loss of meaning from, 78
love of God, *vs.* wrath of God, 3,
35, 57, 125, 129
Luther, Martin, 77

M

Materlinck, Maurice, 119
Mary (mother of Jesus), 64, 77, 93
Assumption of (dogma), 86
Mass, 81-84
meaning, will toward, 2-3
meditation
and prayer, 7-8, 84
techniques of, 13

projection
  archetypes and, 76
  of Messiah/Christ onto Jesus,
    19-20, 71
  religious symbols and, 92
  of Self into messianic expecta-
    tion, 19
  of shadow, 78
  and social attitudes, 39
  of inner darkness and evil into
    world, 6-7, 10, 11, 21-22, 24,
    41, 77, 94, 113-14, 118
Prometheus, 116-17
prophets, 18; *see also individual
  prophets*
Psalm 139, 10, 94
psychoid factor, 70
Psychology and Religion (Jung),
  76, 82, 83

R

rainbow, as sign of covenant, 56,
  120
religious images, 90-99; *see also*
  symbols, religious
religious symbols, *see* symbols,
  religious
"resist no evil," 10, 24, 34, 41-42,
  120
Resurrection, 49
Rilke, Rainer Maria, 101, 105
ritual(s)
  loss of meaning from, 78
  new ones needed, 13
  see also liturgy

S

sacrifice, 83-84
Satan
  cults of, 78
  as part of God, 18; excluded in
    Christian myth, 63
Schaer, Hans: *Religion and the
  Cure of Souls in Jung's Psy-
  chology*, 77
Schell, Jonathan: *Fate of the
  Earth*, 2

seed in earth, parable of, 16
Self, 3-5, 77
  becoming conscious, 80
  and Christ image, 4, 95-96
  darkness in, 77
  and ego, 2, 5, 7, 117; and
    evil in, 94
  God and, 4, 171, 91, 101, 119
  as *imago Dei*, 4, 71, 91
  Jung's rediscovery of, 69-70
  and Kingdom of God within, 4,
    17
  projected into messianic ex-
    pectation, 19
Setluone, Gabriel, 34
shadow, 6-7, 22
  and journey (psychological), 113
  Jung and, 69
  projection of, 78
shepherds, annunciation to, 104
Sibbald, Luella: on polarities in
  movement toward consciousness, 110-12, 116-17, 120-21
Son of man, 19, 60, 79-80
Sonship of Jesus, 49, 50, 59-60,
  65
Spirit, *see* Holy Spirit
"spoons in God's kitchen," 99
substance, Holy Spirit and, 65
suffering
  creative *vs.* meaningless, 113
  of God, 20
symbol *vs.* sign, 92
symbols, religious, 75-87
  adequacy/inadequacy of, 91-94
  conscious relation to, 12-13
  of healing, 127-28
  Jung on, 12, 71
  Jung's own relation to, 99
  need for new ones and new
    meaning in, 45, 76, 96
  as reconciling and integrating, 70
  see also bread and wine; Cross;
    images, religious

T

Teilhard de Chardin, Pierre, 104